INFORMATION AND COMMUNICATION TECHNOLOGY IN EDUCATION

INFORMATION AND COMMUNICATION TECHNOLOGY IN EDUCATION

ISMAIL THAMARASSERI
Lecturer in Education
Farook B.Ed. College Kottakkal
Parappur, Kerala

KANISHKA PUBLISHERS, DISTRIBUTORS
NEW DELHI-110 002

KANISHKA PUBLISHERS, DISTRIBUTORS
4697/5-21A, Ansari Road, Daryaganj
New Delhi -110 002
Phones : 2327 0497, 232 8 8285
Fax : 011-2328 8285
E-mail : kanishka_publishing@yahoo.co.in
kanishkabooks@gmail.com

Information and Communication Technology in Education

First Published-2009

Edition-2022

ISBN : 978-81-8457-130-1

PRINTED IN INDIA

Published by Madan Sachdeva for Kanishka Publishers, Distributors, 4697/5-21A, Ansari Road, Daryaganj, New Delhi-110002, Typeset by Sunshine Graphics, Delhi, and Printed at G.S. Printers, Delhi.

PREFACE

Information and Communication Technologies (ICTs) are a major factor in shaping the new global economy and producing rapid changes in society. Within the past decade, the new ICT tools have fundamentally changed the way people communicate and do business. They have produced significant transformations in industry, agriculture, medicine, business, engineering and other fields. They also have the potential to transform the nature of education-where and how learning takes place and the roles of students and teachers in the learning process.

Teacher education institutions may either assume a leadership role in the transformation of education or be left behind in the swirl of rapid technological change. For education to reap the full benefits of ICTs in learning, it is essential that pre-service and in-service teachers have basic ICT skills and competencies.

The critical factor in the successful integration of ICT into teacher education is the extent to which the teacher educators have the knowledge and skills in ICT integration. A well-conceived and sustained programme of professional development is therefore required to enable the teacher educators and master teachers to develop these skills. This may require development and revision of existing teacher training curriculum guidelines for pre-service and in-service teachers.

The introduction of Information and Communication Technology into the classroom is made changes in the traditional nature of delivering knowledge. Sweeping changes in the modern communication system has made the world as a global village. This book aims to acquint the students/reader with the new trends in information and communication technology. It help to understand the components and factors that effecting information and communication technology. Both teachers and students should understand the use of new trends in ICT in the field of modern education. The use of Internet in education create a new knowledge pattern. Professional education of teachers is reaching new boundaries with the explosion of knowledge. In this book the author has necessarily drawn materials from various sources like standard works and URL's, the names of which have been duly incorporated in the references given towards the end of the chapters. The author shall ever remain obliged to his teachers, parents, friends, colleagues, family members, and students for their directions, guidance and assistance. The author is also great thankful to M/s Infratec Computer Systems, Calicut University for the computerization of the work.

Above all, the author offers his greatful thanks to M/s. Kanishka Publishers, Distributors, New Delhi who came forward willingly to undertake the publishing of this book at a short time.

ISMAIL THAMARASSERI

CONTENTS

1
Computer and Information Communication

Automation in Data Processing

Data

This term is used to describe basic facts about the activities of a business. Data is generally in the form of names, numbers, times, dates, weights, prices, costs, employee names, product names, names of books, schools, students, teachers, roll numbers etc. Data is raw and unprocessed matter or message. Numeric data is consisting numbers alone. Alpha numeric data consists alphabets, numbers and special characters. For example, $, @, % and #.

Information

It is the set of data which has been converted or organized into a more useful or intelligible form. Thus information is obtained by assembling items of data into a meaningful form. For example, where as marks obtained by students and their roll number form the data, and the progress report card. Other forms of information are payslips, schedules, reports, work sheets, bar charts, invoices and account returns. It may be remembered that information may be processed and/or manipulated further to form knowledge.

Data Processing

This term meant for the process of collecting all items of data together to produce meaningful information. Data processing is a term mostly associated with business and commercial work. But it does involve scientific data processing. Data processing varies from being completely manual to those which rely on the use of large electronic computers and accordingly can be:

- Manual -Abaccus, Slide rule, Napiers bone, Logarithms etc.
- Semi-manual-calculator,
- Mechanical- milometer, facit calculator,
- Electronic -Use of digital or Analog computers.

Automation in Data Processing

Automation means the automatic handling of parts between progressive production process. In other words it is the use of automatic equipments in successive stages of production. D.S. Harder had used the term first in 1936. Automation is an automatic system of working. It reduces human action and saves labour. It increases efficiency and speed in operation. Let's discuss the History of Automation in Data processing.

Tools for Counting

Calculating Machines, Punched Card Machines and Computers.

The first instrument for calculation known as 'Abacus' was developed by China in 350 BC. It consisted of beads which were divided into two parts which were movable on the two parts of the rods. The addition and multiplication of numbers was done by using the place value of the digits of the numbers and position of beads in the Abacus. The Abacus was very simple and effective.

The roman device, the calculi, which dates back to 300 BC, is said to have originated from the Greek practice of drawing lines on boards to perform calculations. The stones used for the Roman bead-frame are similar to the stones used for the Abacus in China and Japan. The Abacus is believed to have spread from Rome to China. The Chinese, however, are credited with elaborating on its uses through the rules developed by them in thirteenth century.

Wilhelm Schikard is credited with inventing a calculator in 1623 that could add, substract, multiply and divide. However, only a picture of his invention remained, on the basis of which such a calculator was constructed late last century.

Blaise Pascal, a French Mathematician, wanted to overcome the tedious task of performing calculations by hand, that was imposed on him by his father, a Tax Collector. In 1642, he invented the first well-known Calculator called the Pascaline. Although not a commercial success, it worked well and several models of the device were created.

After this German Mathematician Kummer developed a machine which could do addition and substraction of any number of digits in any order.

The Birth of the Modern Computer

Charles Babbage, British Mathematician, Professor of Cambridge University, imagined a complete computer and to make this imagination true he gave his total life and money. In the year 1822, he succeeded to make a working model of a such machine by which algebric equation and arithmetic tables can be solved and the result was true till the third place of decimal. This machine was named as *Difference Engine.* After this he started to improvise it. In 1842 he presented a new concept of *Analytical Engine* infront of the world. This had most of the all qualities of modern computer. But, he died before this would be completed. He is called the father of modern computer.

His assistant Ada Aaqusta proceed his work. Ada stored instructions in Analytical Engine first time and Analytical Engine worked according to these stored instructions. She is known as the world's first programmer.

After almost 50 years of concept of Charlse Babbage's Analytical Engine, American Scientist Herman Hollerith, who worked in American Census Bureau, developed Electrical Tabulating Machine. In this machine informations were stored with the help of punch cards. These punch cards were put on the tabulating machine and the needles which were mounted in this machine, read the data from the punch cards. When these needles go through the holes of card, they touched the mercury and the electric path was completed. With the help of Herman Hollerith's this machine the work of census, which would be go on about five years completed only two years.

In 1886 Hollerith established a company named Tabulating Machine Company for the business of these machines. In 1911 other companies added to this company. Hollerith named this wide group of all companies Computer Tabulating Recording Company.

In 1924 this company was named as—International Business Machine Corporation (IBM). In 1930s and 1940s different countries like Germany, Britain, USA, Russia were running in the race of computer making. During this period computer techniques processed extremely.

In 1948 Howard A. Aikeb, a Scientist of Harward University, with IBM got success to develop first electronic computer named Automatic Sequence Controlled Calculator. This was named MARC. I.

In 1946, Moore school of Engineering, University of Pennsylvania developed Electronic Numerical Integrator and Calculator (ENIAC).

After it many large computers were made, which did work on binary method and that also had facility of storage. For example, EDUAC, EDSAC, UNIVAC-1, etc.

Computer Generations

First Generation Computer

The first electronic computer came into use at the end of II World War. Development of this machine was started in 1943 and was completed in 1946. This was known as ENIAC (Electronic Numerical Integrator and Calculator) and was designed by Dr. Presper Eckert and Dr. John Mauchley. It contained approximately 18,500 vacuum tubes 70,000 resistors and 10,000 capacitors and weighed about 30 tonnes. It also consumed a large amount of electrical power, considerable space and a large amount of money.

Second Generation Computer

In this generation larger vacuum tubes were replaced with smaller transistors. This major technological advancement was developed by scientists of Bell Laboratories in 1948. This transistors are smaller, reliable and consumed less energy. It reduce the size of computers. Also second generation computers used high level programming languages. Another additional feature was the development of random access storage devices, through which the information could be recorded or retrieved from a storage medium irrespective of the sequential order of the stored information.

Third Generation Computer

It began in 1960, after the invention of Integrated Circuit (IC) or chip. This chip was a one quarter-inch-square piece of material on which thousands of electronic circuits could be implated. This caused the replacement for vacuum tubes, transistors, resistors and capacitors. This is considered to be the backbone of today's modern electronic computers.

Fourth Generation Computer

It was characterized by the development of microprocessor or a microchip in 1970. Approximately 70,000 or more vacuum tube equivalents or transistors could be embedded in single chip of this kind. They were very powerful in terms of the speed of processing and memory. They were otherwise known as "computers on a chip."

Fifth Generation Computer

5th generation computers of 1990's was much faster and more powerful and perhaps intelligent enough to process information and draw conclusions like human beings. Therefore this generation of computer is characterized by "Artificial Intelligence."

Because of the rapid growth of technological advancements in computer no one can predict what the future will bring.

Classification of Computers: By Type and Size

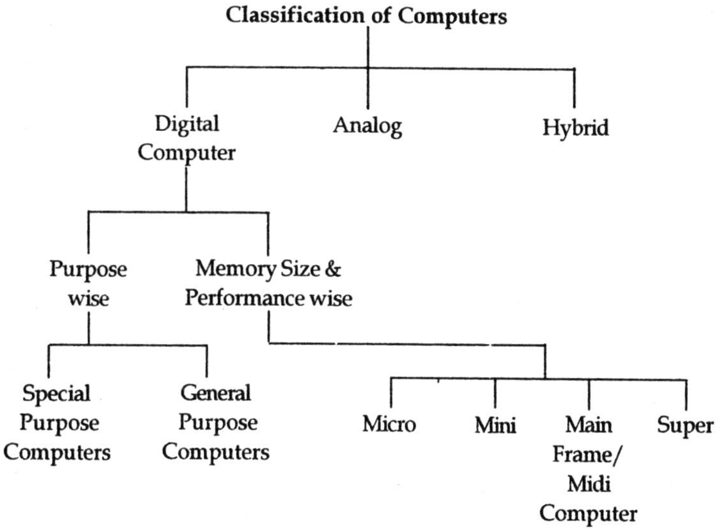

A. Digital Computer

Digital computer can perform only calculations. The mathematical data is represented in the form of Binary Digits (0, and 1). Mathematical calculations are done at high speed. This type of computer can perform only addition. The work of multiplication, division etc. is performed on the lines of addition. Digital computers are widely used for commercial purpose.

Data, which is obtained by counting, is called discrete data. Binary code is used to change signals into digits and digits into signals. A '0' (zero) means there is no voltage or a switch is OFF. A '1' (one) means there is voltage, or a switch is ON.

Eg:- IBM-PC, Apple Computer, Zenith – Macintosh which are used for,

- Counting the total number of students in your class
- Business application
- Scientific application
- Military department.

Digital computers may be further classified in two ways.

1. Purpose wise
2. Memory size and performance wise.

(i) Purpose Wise: These are further divided into two categories:

(a) *Special Purpose Computers:* These are those computers which are designed to carry out a specific task. The instructions to perform the task are permanently stored in the machine. But these type of computers are dealt with specific chores of job and hence are not flexible and resourceful in nature. These computes find their applications in controlling manufacturing process or in communication equipments etc.

(b) *General Purpose Computers:* These are computers which are designed to perform different types of tasks depending upon the different instructions sets fed into it. Since these programmes are to be fed before executing a particular task, it makes workable for almost innumerable applications. Hence it is very versatile in nature.

(ii) Memory Size and Performance Wise: These are further divided into four categories:

(a) *Micro Computers:* It is also known as miniaturized minicomputer. It is a computer whose CPU is microprocessor, i.e., a processor whose all components are on a single Integrated Circuit (IC) chip. These chips are a silicon water about 5mm square and 0.1mm thick with layers of etched and printed circuits containing all the elements required to process binary encoded data.

These computers find their applications in educational training, small business application, etc.

Micro computer is called micro for two reasons, viz.,

1. It is miniature in size (micro means million times less than a unit quantity)
2. It uses micro processor

The family of Laptop computers also belongs to these type of computers. The various examples of these computers may be listed as IBM PC's, Apple Mac, etc. The processors used in these computer come from the family of Intel 8088, 80286, Zilog, Z-80 etc.

(b) *Mini Computer:* It is a small general purpose computer that has computing-power larger than micro-computers. Mini computers are small expensive computers with some what limited input/output capacities. Mini systems are usually designed to simultaneously handle the processing needs of multiple users. Mini-computer provides the facility of more storage capacity and communication link between users. They can also be used as a communication link between, multiple workstations and a central mainframe computer.

Characteristics

- At least 5 times faster than micro computers.
- Designed for 4-8 users in time sharing modes.
- Well support a network of user terminals upto 20.
- They can accept the transfer data from input/output devices at the maximum speed of 4 million bytes/second.
- These systems use Winchester hard disk drives of 80 MB each, 1 or 2 floppy drives and 7 to 8 printers and fixed storage of 160 MB.

Eg: HCL Horizon III
NELCO 5000
Honeywell (XPS-100)

(c) *Mainframe Computers/Midi Computers:* These are large-size computers which occupy a large A/C roomful space and main memory size upto 128 MB. Since all its peripherals are mounted in large cabinet type of frames. It can be used by 128 users simultaneously in time sharing mode.

Characteristics

- These are big general purpose computers capable of handling all kinds of scientific/commercial problems.

- They can accept and transfer data from input/output devices at the rate of millions of bytes/second.
- They can accept all types of high level languages.
- They have large online secondary storage capacities and can support a number and variety of peripheral devices like magnetic tape drives, hard disk drives etc.
- They can support 100 users of a time.
- They have high speed cache (hidden store of something) memory, which enables them to process applications faster than mini or micro computers.

Eg: IBM's 308 x -580 series

DEC 1090
ICL's Series 9
UNIVAC 1100/60

(d) *Super Computers* : Super computers are the most powerful among the digital computers. These are the biggest general purpose computers capable of executing more than 10,000 million instructions per second and have storage capacity of millions bits/chip.

- These are the fastest computers available in the market.
- This type of computer mainly used for designing the wings of super sonic air crafts, world wide weather forecasting, etc.

The high speed in these computers is due to the use of number of microprocessors working in parallel and high storage densities are obtained by using magnetic bubble memories and charge coupled devices.

A super computer CRAY-1 is considered as the most powerful computer today.

PARAM and ANURAG are super computers produced by India. PARAM, developed by CDAC (Centre of Development of Advanced Computer Technology), has exporting to European and American countries. PARAM 9000 is latest in this series. Flowsolver is still another parallel machine produced by India.

In fact, there are about five centers in India which are actively involved in the development of super computers. Eg:- BARC (Bhabha Atomic Research Centre). It has also come out with its own small super computer for their own purpose.

B. Analog Computer

Analog is a Greek word, which means establishing similarities between two quantities. In analog computer, similarities are established in form of current or voltage signal. Analog computers operate by measuring rather than by counting. For example, spedometer of an automobile, flow and temperature measurement in oil refinery, wrist watch, Traffic control light system, controlling machineries.

These type of computers doesn't give hundred-per cent accurate results, but by these computers at most 99 per cent accurate result can be get.

C. Hybrid Computer

The device using desirable features of both analog and digital machine.

For example, Hospital ICU (Intensive Care Unit). It detecting patients heart function and temperature. The function of heart and temperature measurements may be converted in to numbers and supplied to a digital component in the system. This component is used to monitor the patient's vital signs and to send an immediate signal to the doctor's room, if abnormal reading is detected.

Computer System

Computer is a group of integrated parts that have common purpose of performing the operations called for in the programme executed, it qualifies as system. The term *system* is used in many ways. But for computer users, a system is a group of parts that are integrated for the purpose of achieving some objective.

Hardware

A computer system has two basic parts: Hardware and software. The equipment associated with a computer system is the hardware. The physical part of computer or all the visible things related to a computer is called Hardware. In order to function properly, a computer system must have all four types of Hardware: Input, Processing, Output and Storage. The mouse, Joystick, key-board are the input devices, and the monitor and speakers are the output devices. The processor is the processing hardware and hard drive, CD-ROM drive, floppy drive are the storage hardwares.

A computer system is made of three basic units. Input Devices like the key-board and mouse, the Central Processing Unit (CPU) and Output Devices like the monitor screen, printer, speakers etc. The CPU is heart of computer system. Since the processing unit is central, the input and output devices connected to this are called Peripherals.

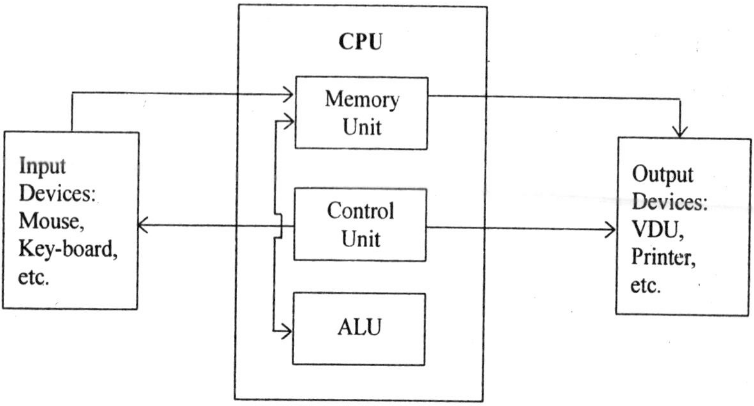

The Block Diagram Showing the Three Units of a Computer

Input Devices

An input device accepts instructions from the user or data from the environment for processing. The function of an input device is to convert the input into a form that the computer accepts. The mouse and key-board are the most widely used input devices. Examples of other input devices are microphone, scanner, barcode reader, etc.

The CPU-Central Processing Unit

The main 'work' of the computer-processing data by arithmetic and logical operations-takes place in the CPU.

The CPU accepts input data, processes it and produces the output information. The CPU also controls operations of other units of the computer. The CPU has three sub-units, namely,

- Memory Unit
- ALU-Arithmetic and Logic Unit and,
- Control Unit.

Memory Unit

Datas and instructions accepted by the computer are stored in the internal memory of the computer before they are processed. The internal memory also called primary memory. This is classified into two.

1. Random Access Memory -RAM
2. Read Only Memory - ROM

RAM is volatile memory. That is temporary memory. As soon as you shut down your computer, or the power goes off for some reason or the other, whatever data stored on the RAM disappears. It is temporary memory, hence it doesn't help store data.

ROM is read only memory. It contains programmes and datas that are permanently recorded when the computer is manufactured. It is read and used by the processor, but cannot be changed/altered by the user.

Different Units of Memory

The units of measurement of memory capacity are bit, byte, KB, MB, GB and TB. Bit is the smallest unit of computer memory. It represents the storage of a binary digit '0' or '1'. It is short form of binary digit.

Byte is the standard unit of computer memory.

8 Bit	=	1 Byte
1024 Byte	=	1 KB - Kilo Byte
1024 KB	=	1 MB - Mega Byte
1024 MB	=	1 GB - Giga Byte
1024 GB	=	1 TB - Tera Byte

Hard Disk

A Hard Disk is a magnetic disk kept inside a sealed unit. This is high capacity storage device encased within the computer system. The storage capacity of the hard disk increasing by every passing day. Hard disks are measured in Gigabytes.

Secondary/Auxiliary/Subsidiary Storage Devices

The devices which are used to storage of information in auxiliary memory are called auxiliary storage devices. Eg:- Magnetic tape, Floppy Disk, CD, Pendrive, etc. The benefits of secondary storage are large space capacity, reliability, convenience, removable, economy.

Arithmetic and Logic Unit (ALU)

Instructions for all basic operations of the computer (Mathematical manipulations and logical operations). Flow from the ALU.

Control Unit

Control Unit manages the functioning of all units in the computer. It co-ordinates flow of data inside the computer. Finally, the control unit directs the flow of results of processing form the memory unit to the output device.

Output Devices

Output devices receive the results of computer processing in the coded form. They convert the results as visual images on the Visual Display Unit (VDU) or as print on papers or a sound coming through speakers, depending on which output device you are using.

Software

All the invisible things related to the computer is called software. These are programmes or instructions. These instructions used to control hardware and accomplish tasks. That makes hardware work for us. Software falls into two broad categories.

1. Application software and
2. System softwares/operating softwares

Application software allows you to perform a particular task or solve a specific problem. Many works can be done by computer. For each work a related programme is to be installed, therefore computer can work according to given instructions. Such programmes which are made to do desired work by computer are called application software.

Eg: Word processors like M.S. Word, Word Perfect, Internet Browsers like Nets Scape Navigator, Microsoft Internet Explorer, Crazy Browser, Designing Software like Adobe Photoshop.

System software/operating software/system is the set of programmes that lies between application softwares and the hardware devices. It is the communication between the user and computer. It is the platform of any computer. In the absence of this software computer cannot be operated. As soon as your computer is turned ON, the operating system software is loaded in order to use your computer devices and other softwares.

Eg: MS. DOS
MS Windows
LINUX's UNIX
Solaris etc.

Years ago we used MS-DOS, this was a command driven programme-in which you needed to know command names and Syntax. The operating software like MS Windows are function with

GUI-Graphical User Interface. A GUI uses graphic symbols, Icons in its Interface. It is user friendly, needn't knowledge on computer languages and commands etc.

Software also classified in another way. That is,

1. Proprietory softwares
2. Free softwares

In proprietary softwares, the source code/base programmes are limited to the manufactor/producer.

Eg: - MS office or MS Windows of Microsoft Corporation.

Free software doesn't mean it is free. But it also give the source code to the user/customer. We have freedom to change the programme. Eg:-LINUX.

Computer Peripherals/Devices/Ports

Graphic Tablet

The graphic tablet is commonly used input equipment. It allows to draw picture on monitor. When you allow pressure on the pad, the spot lights up at a corresponding point on the screen. The cricket commentators often use this device when they describe some finer points on the field or the curving path of a ball. We see this on the T.V.

Key-board

Key-board is the main important device of a computer. The key-board of computer same as the key-board of type writer. 'QWERTY' key-board is commonly used. The key-board is connected to computer through a cable. The cable establishes the relation between computer and key-board. When any 'key' is pressed on key-board, it appears on the monitor.

There are three LED's (Light Emission Deyod) on the upper right side. When the Caps Lock, Num Lock and Scroll Lock put on, then these LEDs blows and when becomes off then these leads extinguishes.

Keys of key-board can be divided in following six categories.

1. Alphabetical Keys—The keys on which all alphabets of English A to Z.
2. Numeric Keys—The keys on which the digits 0-9.
3. Function Keys—On the upper side of the key board F1-F12.

4. Logical Sign Keys – All the keys on which logical signs i.e., <, >, ?, &, \, /, $, ~.
5. Arithmetical Sign Keys – All the keys on which arithmetical signs i.e., =, +, –, ., #, @.
6. Special or Command Keys – All the keys which are used for special works are called special or command keys. These keys can be described in following types.
   (a) *Cursor Control Keys*—The keys on which ←,→,↑,↓ signs exists are called cursor control keys. Besides this other cursor control keys are home, end, Page Up, Page Down. Arrow keys to use to more cursor left, right, up or down by one character.
   Home Key- To move the cursor to the beginning of the line it is on. End Key – To move the cursor to the end of the line it is on. Page Up – To move backward by one page. Page Down – To move forward by one page.
   (b) *Numeric Key Pad*—Numeric key pad stands on the right side of key-board. The keys are just like calculator keys. The work of these keys are controlled by Num Lock. All the keys work as number keys when Num Lock keys is ON and when Num Lock Keys is OFF, then these keys work as cursor control keys.
   (c) *Caps Lock Key*—Once this key is pressed and released all the letters you type will be in capitals, till you release it once again. A green light (LED) on the key board indicates that this keys is active.
   (d) *Shift Key*—When any key is pressed with the shift key then the upper letter or special signs made keys is typed.
   (e) *Enter/Return Key*—(1) This informs the computer the instruction has finished and how that can perform processing according to instruction. (2) Press and release this to start a new line/paragraph.
   (f) *Pause Key*—At the time of working in any programme we gave a such command by which information presents very fastly on monitor screen and we could not read it, then by press the pause key we give instruction to stop therefore we can read presented information. Now to read forward information press any key.
   (g) *Alt and Ctrl Keys*—Used to give short cut commands.

These keys are used in different softwares for different purpose. Eg: Ctrl + Z, Ctrl + Alt + Del, Alt + F4.

(h) *Back Space Key*—To delete/erase the character to the left of the cursor.

(i) *Del Key*—To delete/erase the character to the right of the cursor.

(j) *Insert Key*—This key is used in different softwares for different purpose. Generally insert key is used to insert any graphics, any text.

(k) *Space Bar*—It is the largest key and it lying on the beneath of key board. This space bar is used to make a blank space of single characters.

(l) *Tab*—To set a specific space.

Mouse

It is a mechanical or optical pointing device used to move on screen pointer. The mouse has two or three buttons to signal to the computer the selection of various programme options. When the ball below the mouse rotates, the rotation of the ball the rollers roll on their axis, then by the electronic shaft indicator, produces the electric pulses. It means, when we move the mouse then the electric pulses are produced. These pulses go into the computer memory where according to these pulses, the instructions are send to monitor screen.

When the mouse active and moves, the mouse cursor also moves on the monitor screen. Generally the left button of mouse used for any command. In modern operating systems like Window-2000, the right button used to present a short cut menu.

The shape of mouse pointer changes for different works in different programmes.

Joystick and Games Paddles: Joy stick and Game paddles are input devices. They allow you to put information into the computer. You use joy sticks, say, to move a car around the screen or for similar activities.

Scanner: It applies a light source to image placed on a glass pane inside. The image can be text, picture, drawing or photograph, etc. The light reflects back from the image into the scanner optics. The image is then reconstructed digitally and displayed on the screen. You can now save, increase/decrease size of the image and edit it.

Optical Bar Readers (OBR): The OBR translates the information contained in a barcode into information sensible to CPU. Bar Codes are a series of a black and White lines of various products. They are a digital display of information about a product-including its price, manufacturing date etc. This information cannot be deciphered by the naked eye.

Optical Character Recognition (OCR): This device reads information by recognizing shapes. The instrument used to read the information is called an OCR wand which can read both words and pictures.

Optical Mark Recognition (OMR): This device is used to read marks made by pencil/pen on a sheet of paper.

Magnetic Ink Character Recognition (MICR): It is a sensing device. A typical use of MICR is for reading the numbers at the bottom of a blank cheque.

Magnetic Strips: Magnetic strips are the narrow brown strips found on the back of a credit card. These contain information coded in the form of magnetic marks and are read when the card inserted into the machine that reads it.

Floppy Drive and CD Drive: These are at once input and output devices. By reading information stored on the surface of a floppy/CD, the computer is using these drives or input devices. But when we write information on a floppy/CD for long term storage, we are using these drives as output devices.

VDU/Monitor and Printer: These are the output devices. The Visual Display Unit (VDU) displays what you input into the computer as well as the output of processing. The screen output is called soft output/Softcopy. The printer output is called a *hard copy.* All these input/output devices are connected to the computer through sockets called *ports.*

The key features of a monitor are colour, resolution and size. The computer screen is divided into *pixels* (which are little squares) and figures are depicted by colouring these pixels. The LCD (Liquid Crystal Display) monitors widely using in the place of CRT (Cathode Ray Tube) monitors now-a-days.

There are essentially 3 types of printers:

1. *Dot-Matrix Printers:* These are based on old technology. These are slow and noisy but still popular because of their

durability and low cost. This printer is noisy because it is an impact printer. The print-head, with a carbon tape between itself and the paper, sends out needle-like pins that press upon the paper and print text.

2. *Inkjet Printers:* Spray ink on the paper from a cartridge. The quality of printing is more good and cost-little high in relation to dotmatrix printers. Now-a-days have seen the advent of low cost colour ink jet printers.
3. *Laser Printer:* It is quick and offers high quality printing. A toner is placed on the paper for the ink to form the required image and then through a heating process it, sticks on the paper.

Computer Languages/Programming Languages

A language is a medium of communication. In order to communicate with each other, humans need language like English, Hindi, etc. In the same manner for communicating with the computer, we use computer language called programming language. A Programming Language consists of all the symbols, characters, and usage rules that permits people to communicate with computers. Special codified technique used to inform the instructions, to be executed by computer, to computer is called Computer Programming Language.

Listing of Instructions to be executed by a computer, written in computer understand language is called programming. A programme is a set of logically related instructions that are arranged in a sequence that guides the computer to solve a problem. There are three types of computer programming languages.

- Machine Language
- Assembly Language and
- High Level Language.

Machine Language

It is the fundamental computer programming language. It is only one language, that computer understand directly. In this programming language number system prepared by binary number '0' and '1' is used. Circuit of computer is made in this manner that it rapidly recognizes the machine language and changes it in electrical signals. There are two states of electrical signal-high and low. Number 1 (one) represents 'Yes' pulse or 'high' and number '0' (zero) represents 'No' pulse or 'Low'.

Advantages of Machine Language

- Computer executes it much fastly
- Computer understood directly without any translator

Disadvantages

- Programmer need to memorize the several code numbers
- Programmer should have total knowledge about hardware structure of computer
- Much possibility of mistakes
- Programming with machine language much arduous, typical, hard and time taking job.

So in modern time the work of programming in machine language is negligible.

Assembly Language

To ease the programmer burden, mnemonic operation codes and symbolic addresses were developed in early 1950's. In assembly language on place of machine code, mnemonic codes were used, which can be understood by human-mind easily, such as-LDA (Load), TRAN (Translat), JMP (Jump). From this for each mnemonic code a particular machine code was also decided.

Eg:- In machine language for substraction 1111 is used, if besides this, use of only SUB is easy to remember.

The translation of an assembly code into machine code is done by programme/software stored in computer, this programme is called Assembler.

Advantages

- It gives a little more readability
- More convenient than machine language
- The assembler can automatically detect the grammatical errors in the programme for the programmer.

Disadvantages

- The assembly languages are machine dependent and, therefore, for a new machine of different type, an entirely new set of instructions has to be learnt.
- It may be noted here that the machine language of one type of machine is altogether different from the machine language of other types of machines.

Eg: The machine language of INTEL based machines is different from that of MOTOROLA based machines. Therefore, assembly languages are also different for different machines. Thus, a programme written in an assembly language is machine dependent and will not run on a different machine. Now you clear that both machine and assembly languages are machine dependent and closes to machine. Therefore, these languages are termed as *Low-Level Languages.*

High Level Languages

High level programming languages are the closest to natural languages such as English and therefore are the easiest to programme a computer with. They also provide single instructions to perform complex tasks, which usually need several machine language or assembly language instructions. This was achieved in 1957 with the introduction of *FORTRAN* (Formula Translation), the first - High level language, developed by IBM (International Business Machine) Corporation. Other examples of high level languages are, COBOL, BASIC, PASCAL, PL-1, C, C++.

Since a high level source programme must be translated first into a form the machine can understand, this is done by a software called compiler, which makes the source code as input and produces out put the machine language.

Assembly Language Programme ⟶ Compiler ⟶ Object Code

There are another type of software which does the translation. This is called interpreter have different approaches to translation. Interpreter converts the high level language programme to machine language line by line where as compiler converts the programme when total programme is entered.

Advantages

- Readability.
- Portability-Programmes could be run on different machines with little or no change.
- Easy debugging-Errors could be easily removed.

Disadvantage

Occupies a large memory of computer.

Fourth Generation Languages/ 4GLs

The 3GLs are procedural in nature, contrary to then 4GLs are non-procedural. Thus a big programme of a 3GL may get replaced by a single statement of 4GLs. In 4GLs, user doesn't directly interact with the operating system through commands as was the case in 3GLs. Rather the user interacts with a utility software which is integral part of a 4GL and that in turn interacts with the operating system to get your work done.

For instance, two lines of Fox Pro have an equivalent code of about 100 lines in COBOL. This illustrates the ease and usefulness of 4GLs.

For example, dBASE, III, ORACLE, FOXPRO.

Advantages

- Increased productivity-The programmers productivity increased by 10 per cent.
- Non-procedural-The programmer/user needn't provide the logic to perform a task.
- Need only limited training.

Disadvantages

- Increased memory requirements
- Lack of Flexibility-Programmer's control is limited.

Computer Networks

A computer network is an interconnection of various computer systems located at different places. In computer network two or more computers are linked together with a *medium* (Copper wire, fibre optics, microwaves, communication satellites) and data communication devices (modem, telephone) for the purpose of communicating data and sharing resources. The computers that provides resources to other computers on a network is known as *server*. In the network the individual computers, which access shared network resources, are known as *workstations* or *Nodes*.

Computer Networks may be classified in three broad categories, based on geographical area.

1. Local Area Network–LAN
2. Wide Area Network–WAN
3. Metropolitan Area Network–MAN.

Local Area Network (LAN)

Networks used to interconnect computers in a single room, rooms within a building(s) on one site are called LAN. The transmission medium is normally coaxial cables. People working in LAN get more capabilities in data processing, work processing other information exchange, and sharing of printer, scanner, etc. compared to stand-alone computers. In a LAN, processing takes place at the individual PC workstation, but network and peripheral management functions are centralized and executed at the server.

Characteristics

- Every computer has the potential to communicate with any other computers of the network.
- High degree of inter connection between computers.
- Easy physical connection of computers in a network.
- In expensive medium of data transmission.
- High data transmission rate (100's of MB/second).

Wide Area Network (WAN)

In contrast to LAN, a WAN is spread over a larger geographical area (like across the cities, different locations within a city, across building etc.). The distance between computers connected to WAN is larger. Therefore the transmission mediums are used are normally telephone lines, microwaves and satellite links.

For example,

1. Arphanet of Advanced Research Project Agency of U.S. Department. This network connects more than 40 universities and institutions throughout USA and Europe.
2. The reservation system of Indian Railway.

Characteristics

- *Communication Facility*—Computer conferencing, it saves phone calls.
- *Remote Data Entry*—It means sitting at any location you can enter data, update data and query other information of any computer attached to the WAN but located in other cities.
- *Centralized Information*—This means if a organization/ company is spread over many cities, they keep their important business data in a single place. As the data are generated from different sites, WAN permits collection of this data from different sites and save at a single site.

Metropolitan Area Network (MAN)

This type of network is same as LAN but the area of this network much wide the LAN. In MAN also computers are connected by cable but some where *amplifiers/repeaters* are used. It can be a personal network. For example, Cable T.V. network facility.

Internet/Internetwork

The *Internet* is the interconnection of many different networks, *Internet* refers to a network owned by a single organization for its internal use. In both of these the underlying technology is same. The Internet is often compared to an ocean because of its enormous size. Perhaps that is why people use the term Navigation/surfing if they are browsing the Internet. The Internet is a world wide communication system that is often referred to as the Net/Information Super Highway. It was initially used fore military and academic purposes, it later developed into a business tool. The Internet is often described as 'a network of networks' because all the smaller networks of organizations are linked together into the one giant network called the Internet.

Communication Media used to Connect Computer Networks

In the infancy of telephony, metal wires were the only medium available for interconnecting subscribers in the network. Today the situation is more favourable. Many telecommunication networks consist of a mix of different transmission media. Operators select a medium on the basis of technical considerations, economic aspects and service life of the equipment. Transmission of media roughly grouped into guided media (copper wire and fibre optics) and Unguided media (radio & microwaves).

1. Guided Media

Cables: Metallic cables (in most cases copper) still constitute a very large part of the telecommunications. There are two main types of metallic cable,

- Paired cable and
- Coaxial cable

Paired Cable: The simplest form of paired cable is found in our homes, For example, Telephone wire, a twisted pair consist of two insulated copper wires. The wires are twisted together in a helical form. The purpose of twisting the wire is to reduce electrical interference from similar pairs close by. The cable core is often covered with one or more layer of paper or plastic tape to keep the cable pairs together and to protect the cable. The cable sheath may be made of plastic or metal (lead or aluminium) or of a combination of both, to protect the cable from mechanical damage. Twisted pair cabling come in several varieties.

Coaxial Cable: Coaxial cable consists of a stiff copper wire as the core, surrounded by a insulating material. The insulator is encased by a cylindrical conductor, often as a closely woven braided mesh. The outer conductor is covered in a protective plastic sheath.

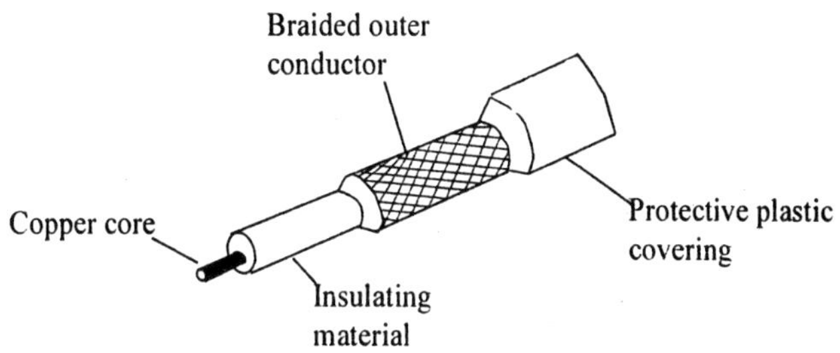

The coaxial tube has very high transmission capacity. Today coaxial cable is no longer installed in the trunk part of the telecommunications network. It replaced by optical fibre cable. Even coaxial cables today using in local data networks, Cable-TV net works and as a feeder for radio antennas.

Optical Fibre

In the 1870's an Englishman, Tyndall showed that light can be conducted through a bent jet of water. At the end of the 19th century, Graham Bell designed an optical telephone. The first field trial with optical cable were carried out in 1975. In 1980, the first commercial systems were opened for telephone traffic. The optical fibre is used primarily in urban networks and for long-distance connections mainly for digital transmission. It has a enormous transmission capacity. The interface between Electrical and Optical tranmission requires E/O converters.

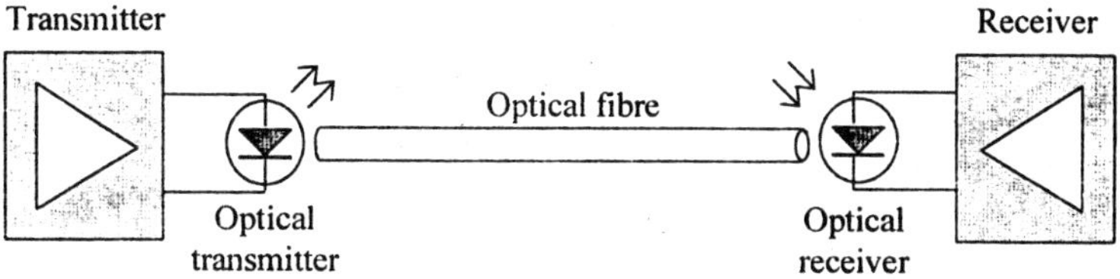

E/O Converters

An optical transmission system has three components. The light source, the transmission medium and the detector, by attaching a light source to one end of an optical fiber and a detector to other end. It has a unidirectional data transmission system that accepts an electrical signal, converts and transmits it by light pulses, and then converts the outputs to an electrical at the receiving end.

Fibre optics cables are similar to coaxial cables, except without the braid. At the centre is the glass core which light propagates. Next comes a plastic jacket to protect the cladding. Fibres are typically grouped together in bundles, protected by an outer sheath.

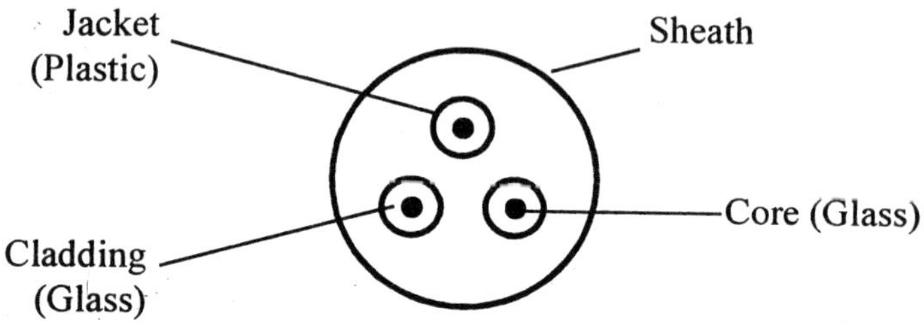

Advantages/Characteristics

- Very high capacity.
- Long repeater spacing—repeaters are needed only about every 30 KM on long lines, versus about every 5 KM for copper.
- Small cable dimension.
- Fibre is lighter than cable—i.e., low weight.
- Small bending radius.
- No cross-talk-fibre do not leak light and are quite difficult to tap.
- Immunity to electromagnetic interference—Electrons in a copper wire affect one another and are themselves affected by electrons out side the wire. Photons in a fibre do not affect one another because they have no electric charge.

2. *Unguided Media*

Mobile phone, Laptop, Palmtop and wrist watch computer users are function without guided medias. For these users wireless communication is the answer. The different types of unguided medias are Radio waves and satellite systems.

Radio Transmission

Radio waves is a transmission medium with large field of applications, and a medium that provides the user with great flexibility. For example, cordless telephones. Radio waves are easy to generate, can travel long distances. Radio waves are omni directional (they travel in all direction from the source). The radio spectrum is divided into eight frequency bands from VLF (Very Low Frequency) to EHF (Extremely High Frequency). The propagation of radio wave depends on its frequency. Radio waves with low frequency used for maritime radio, telegraphy and telex traffic. High frequency radio waves are used for TV broadcasting, and mobile telephony.

Microwave Transmission

Unlike radiowaves, microwaves travel in straight line and do not pass through buildings well. Microwaves have higher frequency than radiowaves. Microwaves communication is so widely used for long-distance telephone communication, cellular telephones, television distribution and other uses.

Infrared and Millimeter Waves

Unguided infrared and millimeter waves are widely used for short range communication. The remote controls used on Televisions, VCR, CD Player and sterios all use infra red communication. They are relatively directional, cheap, and easy to build, but have a major draw back; they do not pass through solid objects.

Satellites

Satellites used for telecommunication are placed in geostationary orbits in the equatorial plane 35,800 KM above the earth's surface. Approximately one third of the earth's surface is covered by an antenna with global radiation. Satellite links are used in national as well as International Telecommunication Networks. The transmission properties of satellite links are excellent and problems are few. INTELSAT (International Telecommunications Satellite Organization) is responsible for the launching and operation of satellites, has in excess of 100 operators as stakeholders.

MODEL QUESTIONS

1. *(a)* A list of input devices is given below:
   - *(a)* Key- board
   - *(b)* MICR
   - *(c)* OMR
   - *(d)* Scanner
   - *(e)* Joystick
   - *(f)* Touch screen

   (b) Select most appropriate one for the following situation:
   1. A person wants to place his own photograph as the desktop wallpaper of his computer.
   2. Children for playing computer games commonly use this device.
   3. For evaluation of objective type of examination.
   4. A person wants to select an item from the display unit.
2. Differentiate between computer hardware and software? Support your answer with examples.
3. Draw the block diagram to illustrate the basic organization of a computer system and explain the functions of various units.
4. What are peripheral devices? Explain any two.
5. How will application softwares help the school administration?
6. Write the advantages of different application softwares used in education system.
7. Explain the characteristics of third generation computers.
8. What is the difference between compiler and interpreter?
9. Explain the following terms:
   - *(a)* E-mail
   - *(b)* news groups
   - *(c)* Remote login
   - *(d)* File transfer
10. What are the functional units of a computer?

REFERENCES

1. Abdu, V.K. (1999). *Computer Lokam (Malayalam)*. Kozhikode: IPH.
2. Das, K.S. (2005). *A Textbook of Information Technology*. New Delhi: Dominant Publishers.
3. Goel, H.K. *Teaching of Computer Science*. Meerut: R. Lall Book Depot.
4. Government of Kerala, Department of Education (2007). *Information Technology*-I, Thiruvananthapuram.
5. Hoole, H.S. *et al.*, (2005). *Information and Communication Technology for Teachers*. New Delhi: Foundation Books.
6. Jain, V.K. (2001). *Computer for Beginners*. Delhi: Pustak Mahal.
7. Mallik, U. (2002). *Learning with Computers*. New Delhi: NCERT.
8. Nochad, A. & Shanavas. *Information and Communication Technology*. Calicut University: Shaan Vishaal.
9. Rajasekar, S. (2004). *Computer Education and Educational Computing*. Hyderabad: Neelkamal Publications (P) Ltd.
10. Singh, J. & Singh, K. *Computer Education*. Ludhiana: Tandon Publications.

2

Information Technology

The Concept of Information Technology

As the twenty-first century ushers in the information age, we will experience new ways of living and working. IT includes all the various activities connected with the location, acquisition, processing, storage and communication of information. IT deals with all the information activities. It is concerned with computing, micro-electronic and telecommunication equipment which make the location, processing and transfer of information possible in the shortest possible time.

A near-synonymous term of IT is Information Science, but there exists some differences. Information Science in turn is transformed into IT when extensive use of mechanical, electronic or micro-electronic equipment is made in the processing and communication of information, so that no time is lost in transferring the technology to users after it has been generated.

Thus the extensive use of telephone, radio, television, satellite transmission, computer, microprocessor etc. transformed information science of yesterday into information technology.

Towards Information Technology

In the field of education, large scale merging with ICT's has taken place. IT made classroom interaction very effective.

Science and Technology is responsible for 'Information Explosion'.

Enormous manpower is engaged in scientific and technological research; and the output of this research is say as increase of new information. It is experienced that the conventional methods of storing/retrieving information is quite inadequate.

Computer application helps in the storage/retrieval of the vast and ever increasing information.

Through central processing and storage, any information centre can access the information from all over the world via terminals. As such, it is now not necessary for each information centre to collect, organize and store information by itself.

Technologies Influencing Information Communication

The progress in the fields such as,

- Microprocessors.
- Storage and memory technology.
- Communication technologies.
- Reprographic-reproduction of documents.
- Micrographic technology-all types of micro documents transparent/opaque or in roll or sheet.

These are contributed much to the major technological advancement that are influencing Information and Communication Technology.

Microprocessors

The invention of microprocessors in 1970's reduced the size of the computers and increased its capacity for performance.

The advent of microprocessors has led to various trends in information processing design.

They are:

1. Specialized High Performance Auxiliary Processors—To add specialized functions to the general purpose computers.
2. Processor Mimics—In the form of processor in mini-computers that are suitable with large system in efficiency for performance.
3. Multi-Processor Systems—With distributed responsibilities and a network of data sharing arrangement in a single system.
4. Personal Computer Phenomenon—Making home computer possible, which is an important step towards personal information system.

Storage and Memory Technologies

Advancement in storage and memory technology is another aspect that is favourable to ICT. In the place of 1.44 MB floppy disks, today 8 GB pen drives and memory cards available.

Optical memories are alternate mass storage devices with huge capacity and these have paved the way for the development of a new low cost storage technology. In optical storage devices, the information is written using laser beam. The optical memory devices which are now become increasingly popular.

Eg: CD – Rom (Compact Disk Read Only Memory).

DVD – (Digital Video Disk)-more storage capacity than CD

MP3 – (MPEG Layer 3)
It is a file format for compressing digitalized audio files.

MPEG – Motion Picture Coding Expert Group. A committee of international standard organization which develops format for compressing digitized audio/ video files.

Information Technology in India

Computerization has made significant progress in India. Information Technology (IT) and Information Technology Enabled Services (ITES) made drastic changes in India. New areas being promoted, viz.,

- Printing, reprography, publishing
- Switching technology
- Remote sensing
- Oil exploration
- Meteorology-study of motions and phenomena of atmosphere
- Climatology
- Data communication
- Information system
- Education
- Research etc.

Indian Statistical Institute (ISI) Calcutta was the first establishment installed computer system (HEC-2M) in India in 1958. ISI also developed the first indigenous computer in 1964. During the period 1955-64 India installed 16 computers, out of which 10 were from the IBM. During 1964-72 around 170 computer systems were installed. Out of these 75 were supplied by the IBM. The share of the private companies was 45 per cent of the market during this period. The private players entry restricted by Ministry of Labour and Rehabilitation. The positive result of this that Electronic Corporation India Ltd., ECIL, Hyderabad capture local market, with liberal financial backup from government.

1990 onwards as a result of LPG (Liberalization, Privatization, Globalization) the picture is utterly changed. Many private companies enter to the field and traditional companies and investors also turn to Information Technology and Information Technology Enabled Services.

National Informatic Centre (NIC)

The NIC was established in 1975, with aim to improve the productivity in the working of the government.

Purposes

- To stream line the information base, systems analysis of the organization structure.
- Qualitative studies feeding the planning process.
- Evolving an effective Management Information System (MIS) for the Ministries and Departments of the Government of India.
- Demonstrate the benefits of computerization to the Government Departments.

Methodologies

1. Interactive management information system.
2. Processing of data sources.
3. Standardization in coding and formats.
4. Correlatory data bases.
5. Spreading the effects of innovation.

NICNET is a network established by NIC.

NICNET—National Informatic Centre Net Work

NICNET was commissioned in 1977. Through NICNET around 200 technical personnel are serving over 40 Ministries and Departments of the Government of India and their associated organizations, they spread out in Delhi.

More than 150 databases have been created for various user organizations. All these computers at the districts, state and regional head quarters and Delhi will form a wide network.

INDONET

The INDONET is a commercial data network installed by Computer Maintenance Corporation (CMC) of the Department of Electronics, Government of India.

Purposes

- Distributed data processing
- Software export
- Bank computerization
- Computer consultancy

INDONET covers entire India by setting up five computer nodes at Mumbai, Delhi, Kolkatta, Chennai and Hyderabad and making these accessible from all parts of the country.

Regional Computer Centres

Regional computer centres were introduced to promote computerization in the country. Two regional computer centres set up at the Jadavpur University, Calcutta (1977) and Chandigarh in 1979. These centres conducted advanced computer courses, seminars and workshops.

Centre for Development of Advanced Computing (C-DAC)

The C-DAC is a non-profit, application oriented, Research and Development (R&D) Institution of Excellence under Ministry of Communication and Information Technology, Government of India. C-DAC dedicated to the development of electronic products and systems.

The mandate given to C-DAC is to generate manpower to meet the growing demand for trained manpower.

Institutions Under C-DAC

- Advanced Computing Training School (ACTS)
- C-DAC School of Advanced Computing, Mauritius.
- Programme for Advancing Computer Education (PACE)
- National Multimedia Resource Centre (NMRC)

These institutions offering variety of courses/programmes.

National Centre for Software Development and Computing Techniques (NCSDCT)

NCSDCT set up at the Tata Institute of Fundamental Research (TIFR) Mumbai in 1974. It aims development of software tools and computing techniques.

Major Areas of Operation

- Software engineering
- Computer networking
- Graphic-Oriented Computer-Aided Design (CAD)

Computer Maintenance Corporation (CMC)

The CMC functioning under the Department of Electronics, Government of India. CMC provides maintenance support to all the computer systems available in India.

It's service includes,

- hardware maintenance
- site preparation
- installation and commissioning of systems
- consultancy
- software development
- system integration and enhancement
- education and training.

Computer Training Programmes and Instructional Programmes in India

In India Educational Broadcasting begins during 1964. SITE (Satellite Instructional Television Project Experiment) take first step on the same in 1975-76. SITE's educational programmes produced by *Doordarshan* and telecasted by ISRO.

In 1983 INSAT IB (Information Satellite) broadcaste daily 2.45 hours in morning for primary schools and 2 hours for adults in evening through television.

University Grants Commission-UGC launched the project CWC (Country Wide Classroom) on August 15, 1984. UGC provide TV sets and they produce ETV (Educational Television) programmes.

In 1986 MCA programme was started by several universities as reported in the Programme of Action (POA) of National Policy on Education-(NPE) 1986. Diploma and short term programmes were started widely.

At school level various computer literacy programmes were started. Eg:- For example, CLASS (Computer Literacy and Studies in School).

EDUSAT (Educational Satellite)

It is the artificial satellite launched by Government of India exclusively for educational purpose on 20th September 2004.

EDUSAT-Functions

- provide quality education
- promot self-learning method
- utilize digital library facilities
- provide an interactive learning environment
- make available the classes of experts, resource persons to all
- maintain equality of educational opportunities.

Indian Information Technology Act

IT ACT provides legal recognition for transactions carried out by means of electronic data interchange and other means of electronic communication.

It related to the use of alternatives of paper-based methods of communication and storage of information.

It facilitate electronic filing of documents.

The Act contains 94 sections in 13 chapters. The 91-94 sections are related the amendments to the existing acts/codes are,

1. Amendments to the Indian Penal Code (1860)
2. Amendment to the Indian Evidence Act (1872)
3. Amendments to the Bankers Books Act (1891) and
4. Amendment to the Reserve Bank of India Act (1934).

Information Technology in Kerala

Technopark, Trivandrum

Technopark, Trivandrum an autonomous society promoted by the Government of Kerala. It is the Indias first technology park and among the three largest IT parks in India today. Technopark hosts over 120 IT and ITES companies, employing over 15,000 IT professionals. Technopark provides world class infrastructure and low cost IT environment.

Technopark Software Engineering Competency Centre (TSECC) in association with IBM, where free access to cutting edge software engineering tools is compined with expert hand holding.

Technopark Business Innovation Centre (T-BIC) incubating successful knowledge enterprises.

'IT@School'

IT@school, a project for achieving excellence and equity of educational opportunities through the use of IT. "*Excellence and Equity in Education – No exceptions – No excuses*" this is the vision statement of the IT@school. It is the project of Government of Kerala to introduce IT-enabled teaching/learning in the high schools of the state.

In April 2000 the Government of Kerala constituted an IT task force for developing a vision for the use of IT in education. The vision has been outlined in the document "IT in Education – Vision 2010."

The document envisions a total transformation of the classroom at all levels. IT acts as a powerful driving in this transformation.

Aims

- IT to be introduced to high school curriculum
- IT to be used as a tool for improving the quality of teaching/learning
- IT to be taught as a curricular subject.

The Uniqueness of IT@School

- Winner of National e-governance award 2006 for exemplary leadership and ICT achievements.
- Government made IT, a compulsory subject in school curriculum. About 40,000 computers have been supplied to the schools.
- The first state to conduct compulsory IT examination in SSLC examination.
- Nearly 16 lakh students per year benefited in acquiring IT skills.
- Manpower includes 161 master trainers and about 5600 IT co-ordinators.
- Training imparted to all high school teachers. About 60,000 teachers trained in IT.
- 'IT mela' introduced to encourage IT initiatives among teachers/students.
- Hardware made available in a totally decentralized way providing assistance under Local Area Development (LAD) funds of MP/MLA, Local Self Governments (LSG), Parent Teacher Associations, Alumni's etc.
- Developed its own Operating System (OS) in Linux.

- Infrastrucutre development in schools-supply of Generator, multimedia room etc.
- Introduction of EDUSAT network and VICTERS.

Edusat Initiatives

- IT@school is the nodel agency for implementing EDUSAT initiating in Kerala.
- IT@school runs two channels of EDUSAT,
  1. Interactive channel
  2. Non-interactive channel-VICTERS
- There are a total of 95 Satellite Interactive Terminals (SIT's) and full fledge utilization of interactive network.
- ROTs (Read Only Terminal) supplied in 1400 schools for reception of VICTERS channel.

'AKSHAYA'

It was the first district-wide E-literacy project in India. It firstly started in Malappuram district Kerala.

Through a network of over 600 village telecentres (E-centres) Akshaya has conducted one of the world's largest-computer literacy drives. The process of implementing Akshaya to all over Kerala is going on.

Akshaya facilitating the widespread use of ICT by all segments of Kerala Society. It ensuring the dissemination of the benefits of IT among people.

Benefits of 'Akshaya'

- Provision of Computer Literacy to at least – one person in every home.
- Development of 6000 Akshaya centres to provide ICT access to the entire state population.
- Provision of convenient access for the common man to information services with in two kilometers.
- Ensuring Socio-Economic Empowerment of Local Community.
- Enhancement of quality of IT infrastructure available in the State.
- Extension of the IT infrastructure to the rural areas.
- Generation of 50,000 direct employment opportunities.
- Generation of direct investment of over Rs. 500 crores.

E-GOVERNANCE

Electronic Governance (E-governance) means the delivery of government services/information to the public using electronic means.

Use of IT by government facilitates an, efficient, speedy and transparent process for dissemmating information to the public/ agencies.

E-governance is the use of ICT's by public sectors with the aims of,

- Improving information and service delivery
- Encouraging peoples participation in decision making
- Making governance more accountable, transparent and effective.

The main goal of E-governance is to promote democracy by ensuring effective governance by the Government.

Effective governance includes,

- Improved government decisions
- Increased faith of citizens in government
- Increased government accountability and transparency
- Ability to accommodate the public will
- Increased involvement of stakeholders, (NGO's, business concerns) and interested citizens in novel strategies adopted for meeting public challenges.

MODEL QUESTIONS

1. As a teacher how will you effectively utilize the potentials of educational broad casting?
2. List the educational services of EDUSAT.
3. Explain the role of communication satellites in Non-formal education.

REFERENCES

1. Arora, A. *A Complete Book on B.Ed. Information Technology*. New Delhi: Cyber Tech Publications.
2. Das, S.K. (2005). *A Textbook of Information Technology*. New Delhi: Dominant Publishers and Distributors.

3

Communication Technologies Changes and Challenges

Technological Change

There are tremendous changes are visible in the field of Information and Communication Technology during these periods viz.,

- Replacement of analog equipment by digital systems.
- Digital revolution.
- Convergence of the computer, telecommunication, and audio-visual industries.
- Wide range of innovations leading to the convergence of various techniques.

Convergence

Integration of customer end terminal equipment/access devices such as the telephone, television and personal computer.

The accelerating progress in Information and Communication Technology (ICT) is based on three fundamental changes, viz.,

- The digitization of images, sound and data
- Digital data compression
- The growing power of electronic components.

1. Digital Revolution

Digital revolution means progress in micro-electronics, digitization of images, sounds and datas. In conventional analog systems were converted into electrical signals. With digitization the same signals coded in to strings of numbers. But they extremely demanding transmission capacity. Digital compression can solve this difficulty.

2. Digital Compression

Transmission of multimedia materials in uncompressed mode is very difficult. The only remedy is massive compression. This situation leads to research on compression technologies.

All compression systems require two algorithms; one for compressing the data and another for decompressing. This is referred as encoding and decoding. Digital compression reduce the time and cost of data transmission, without decrease the quality of content.

For example, MP3 (MPEG Layer 3)

When the decoded output is not exactly equal to the original input, the system is said to be *lossy*. If the input and output are identical, the system is *lossness*.

3. Growing Power of Electronic Components

Gordon Moore, one of the founder of INTEL observed in 1965, "Microprocessor power doubles every 18 to 24 months." This statement is still true.

The power and performance of semi conductors doubles almost-2 years, with a corresponding drop in their price.

Each new processor launched on the market contains approximately many transistors as contained by its predecessor.

The progress in the field of hard disk is also noteworthy. In 1956, RAMAC 305 (Random Access Method of Accounting and Control) one of the first hard disk store 5 million byte.

In 1997, the IBM hard disk *Travel Star VP* has a storage capacity of 1.5 million GB of data.

The reducing of size and enhancement of components and memories are on going process. That makes the system smaller, faster, powerful, less expensive. The low cost computers available in the present market is an example to this.

These technological changes have resulted the convergence of telecommunications, computer and audio-visual technologies, which were previously separated.

Changes in Media Environment

Today we feel a drastic change in the media environment. That resulted,

- Increasing number of information media, both print and visual.

- Non-stop growth in the range of programmes.
- Specialized magazines, journals and periodicals.
- Local radios, private FM radio providers.

These resulted in new behaviour patterns like fragmented listening and reading. New technical resources, publishers, and broad casters have found vastly enhanced means of reaching their target audience.

The technological advances lead to upheals in the media landscape. Traditional geographical divisions have given way to wide range of markets.

The computerization made a revolutionary impact on Journalism, it create new jobs and change the old. As a result of digital revolution newspapers provide their online editions on the net.

1. Radio-TV Broadcasting

In Radio market, broadcasters have taken of the new transmission systems,

- To diversify the programmes and
- To improve listening comfort

The trend now being adopted is to provide high-fidelity digital satellite programmes.

F.M. (Frequency Modulation) Trend

F.M. technology discovered by American Scientist Edwin Amstrong. Around 300 new radio stations sanctioned to start in India. In this, 17 numbers are in Kerala. Viz.,

- Radio Mango of Manorama Group
- Club FM of Mathrubhumi Group
- S.F.M. of Sun T.V.
- Radio Mirchi of Times of India Group
- Big FM of Reliance and Asianet Adlab.

The newly sanctioned FM stations only broadcast leisure, entertainer programmes, no right to broadcast news programmes. A particular percentage of revenue get to Government. The New FM stations are utilizing the Prasarbarathi/ Akashavani amenities and facilities and a share of revenue given to them.

In the television sector, data digitization technique led to,

- Vast increase in the programmes.
- Qualitative improvements both in pictures and sound.
- Possibility for interactivity
- More live programmes.

2. ***Change in Press Work***

Computerization made drastic changes in the press work, viz.,

- Everywhere to type their own articles, enter, copy, edit- to a computer system.
- Replaced traditional type setters.
- Manual mounting of pages disappears.
- Computer assisted page make-up. Eg: Use of Adobe Page Maker, etc.
- Automation in printing sequence.
- Number of staffs (typographers, graphic artists, photo engravers) considerably reduced.

3. ***Fax Transmission***

As a result of progress in telecommunications and satellites, a variety of items such as texts, photographs and graphics can be transmitted now by an exact copy from one continent to another. This technique is being widely used in press work.

Newspaper production is now fully controlled by computer.

Fax facsimile: Electronic transmission of a document from one point to another.

4. ***The Internet and the Press***

The first attempt on electronic publishing was in 1992 by the daily newspaper the *San Jose Mercury News. Deepika, the Malayalam* newspaper first start internet edition. Secondly *Deshabhimani* and it popularized/sensationalized by *Malayala Manorama.*

Internet editions enabled the readers possessing computer facility to access electronic edition any where in the world at any time.

Foundations for Information Society

1. ***Satellite Networks***

The first communication satellite was launched in 1962. A communication satellite contains several transponders,

- Amplifies the incoming signal and

- Broadcasts it at another frequency with a view to avoid Interference.

The downward beams can be broad, covering a substantial fraction of the earth's surface.

The earlier satellites (before 1989) were low-or mid power systems, its outputting signals reception required large scale dish antenna. After the use of high power satellites the size of dish antennae reduced.

The new generation satellites are radically increase the supply of interactive services.

2. Cable Networks

Mainly three types of cables are used in cable networks. Viz.,

- Twisted pairs
- Co-axial cables
- Fibre optics.

Two kinds of communication (Fibre optics and wireless) are popular today.

3. Digital Terrestrial Network

The Concept Digital Terrestrial Network developed by Federal Communication Commission (FCC) USA. It was initially designed for High-Definition Television (HDTV).

In the new technology a specific digital microwave transmitter with the range of 5 to 10 kms broadcasts the pictures. In surrounding villages or rural areas a small receiver antenna can distribute the signals to between 10-15 households.

4. Mobile Networks

We feel mushroom growth in the mobile phone sector. It is popularized because of its 'mobile' nature.

Mobile radio telephones were first used for Maritime and Military communication during the beginning of the 20th century.

In 1946, the first system for car-based telephones was setup in St. Louis.

In the 1960's IMTS (Improved Mobile Telephone System) was installed. IMTS supported 23 channels spread out from 150 MHz to 450 MHz. Due to the small number of channels, users often had to wait for a long time before to get a dial tone.

In 1982 Bell Labs, USA invented AMPS (Advanced Mobile Phone System). In AMPS the geographical area divided into cells. At the centre of each cell there is a base-station consists of a computer and transmitter/receiver, connected to an antenna. All the base stations are connected to a single device called on MTSO (Mobile Telephone Switching Office) or MSC (Mobile Switching Centre). The channel capacities of the AMPS are very compared to that of IMTS.

The mobile communication market has one of the highest expansion ratio in the telecommunication sector, with an annual growth rate nearing 20 per cent.

The Liberalization, Privatization, Globalization (LPG) and New Economic Policy during 1990's has resulted in the granting of licenses to the private operators and that leads to an unimaginable growth in this sector.

5. *Information Highways*

Information Highways means a high speed global network capable of routing to subscribers, at high speed, a series of new interactive services (distance learning, data bank quering, teleshoping, telemedicine, pay-per-view television, picture phoning).

These can be the basis for a true technological, economic, and cultural revolution and it eliminate all geographical, temporal and cultural frontiers.

It is not a single physical network but a series of local, regional, national and international infrastructures linked to form a world wide information highway.

Information Highways will lead to far reaching changes, particularly in the sectors of creative art, education, adult training, health, culture, etc. Information highways become a focal point of political, industrial and cultural issues. For example, Tehalka.com. But in other side, this revolution make people more wider than closure. It develops individualism and deteriorating real friendship.

6. *The Internet*

The Internet is a huge collection of computer networks that can communicate with each other-a network of networks.

What are the Applications of Internet?

- E-Mail: The ability to compose, send, receive electronic mail.

- News Groups: News groups are specialized forums in which users with a common interest can exchange messages.
- Remote Login: Using Telnet, R-login or other programmes, users anywhere on the internet can log in to any other machine on which they have an account.
- File Transfer: Using FTP (File Transfer Protocol) programme. It is possible to copy files from one machine on the internet to another.

Till 1990 internet used mainly by academics, government and researchers. The text transmission only possible upto this. After the application of www (world wide web)- invented by Tim Berners Lee internet highly popularized. Www made possible pictures, text, sound, video, linking and more. Today approximately 60 per cent of internet transactions made for trade and 27 per cent for research, 9 per cent for administration and less than 5 per cent for education.

Economic Change and Information Technology

Characteristics of Modern Economy

- It is knowledge based.
- It is growth based.
- The triumph of software over hardware.
- Anything can be made if proper knowledge about that, made available.
- Free from conventional constraints of distance and scarcity of resources.
- Digital technology and data compression have produced means of creating information.
- Information multiplied to infinity.
- Growing production of paper less goods like softwares.
- Development of "know-how."

Even strategic resources we get from internet

- Transforming of economy into a knowledge based entity.
- Software industry over take manufactures of hardware.

On the global IT market, the value of software and related services equalled that of hardware, as evidenced by sales of almost $ 200 billion out of a total market worth $ 380 Billion.

Development strategies around the world now invest in knowledge, education and training, they being the keys to success in economic development.

In the developed countries jobs and professions are undergoing deep changes affecting every single aspect concerning the work place. The traditional concepts of office space, time, structure etc. utterly changing today. '24x7' approaches, 'Individualization', 'Marrying the Profession', 'Double Income No Kids'-(DINK) families, 'Action Leads Satisfaction' 'You are the Boss' etc. are the mottos and characteristics of new generation jobs.

Employment is increasingly concentrated in the production of paperless goods and the supply of services.

Creation of new jobs in services that utilize new Information Technology.

Eg: Teleshoping, BPO (Business Process Out Sourcing) Jobs, online trading, Telemarketing, etc.

The globalization of economic activities has resulted in enhanced concentration in the communication sector, strong growth in the world market for new IT and acceleration of development of electronic commerce (E-commerce).

The very nature of web and its capacity for digital data transmission make the internet a prime channel for trade in any paperless product or service.

Now, we can conclude that the backbone of the current economic change is Information and Communication Technology and its accessories.

Media Globalization and Regulations

The term 'Globalization' means integration of economies and societies through cross-country flows of information, ideas, technologies, goods, services, capital, finance and people. It is multi-dimensional including cultural, social, economic and political dimensions.

Media globalization is also a part of this phenomenon.

For example,

- The development of cross border TV stations and channels
  - TV5, BBC-public service systems
  - Star TV, super channel-private internet/ general channels
  - CNN, Euro News-specialized in news casting channels
  - Euro Sport, Screen Sport-sports channels
  - Disney, Pogo - leisure channels

- MTV, MCM - music channels
- Fashion TV, Trends -life style channels

- They reach millions of homes world wide via cable network/ individual reception of satellite signals.
  - DISH TV, TATA SKY, DD-DTH, BIG TV, SUN DIRECT, etc.
- In order to over come the language obstacles and increase their audience they are investing increasingly in national language programmes.
- TV stations/channels one basically financed by commercials.
- In addition to commercials, some channels obtain a growing share of their revenue from pay-per-view systems. For example pay programmes like Dish TV's 'Movie on Demand'.

Media Regulations

What's the Need of Regulations?

Regulations is the means of reconciling the economic interventionism of public authorities and the market forces in the audio-visual field. In Indian scenario the reason behind the regulation is the radical changes during 1980's. During this period monopolies held by national broadcasting channel Doordarshan. But emergence of private operators and rapid growth of their numbers change the traditionalities. Asianet—first private channel in Kerala start this boom. Tremendous changes in Tamil Nadu leads Political utilization of the channels. Each political party started to a channel for their political propaganda.

New possibilities of transmission like digital broadcasting and emergence of multimedia groups like serial and other allied programme produces, sub businesses, advertisement agencies also come to reality. Ultimately this resulted in enhancing the importance of private interest in the audio visual field. In order to cope with these new up heals some states have drafted a number of laws/regulations.

Different countries have different approaches to the regulations on telecommunications and visual/audio industries. Why? In USA the regulatory agency/body called FCC—Federal Communication Commission. FCC covered the vast area of regulations of the telecommunication and audio-visual stores. In other countries, the two branches of communication are governed separately. The authority for regulation rests with the Office Telecommunication (Oftel) and the Independent Television Commission (ITC). Telecom

Regulatory Authority of India (TRAI) is a governing body functions in India.

Freedom of Information

Freedom of Information is related to Human Rights. It is the basis and criterion for the analysis and interpretation of International laws concerning the media.

Its first consecration occurred in 1789 with the French Declaration of the Rights of man and of the citizen, Article XI of the Declaration asserts that "the free communication of ideas and opinion is one of the most precious rights of man", and that in consequence every citizen can freely speak, write and print, subject to responsibility for the abuse of this freedom in cases determined by law.

In 1946 the UNO recalled in its resolution 59 that "freedom of information is a fundamental human right and is the touch stone of all the freedoms to which the UNO is consecrated." On 10th December 1948 freedom of information was enshrined in the Universal Declaration of Human Rights (UDHR).

Article 19 of UDHR stated, "Everyone has the right to freedom of opinion and expression; this right includes freedom.... to seek, receive and impart information and ideas through any media and regardless of frontiers." UNESCO's Article 11 para 2 (a) deals with the international agreement designed 'to promote the free flow of ideas by word and image'.

After that the general conference of the UNESCO at its 25th session in November 1989-adopted a 'new communication strategy' aimed at meeting the needs of the growing democratics and the developing countries alike. Its goals were three fold:

1. Encouraging the free flow of information, at international as well as national level.
2. Promoting the wider and better balanced circulation of information without any obstacle to freedom of expression.
3. Developing all the appropriate means of strengthening communication capacities in the developing countries, in order to increase their participation in the communication process.

In respect of the first prong of this 'new communication strategy', UNESCO reasserted the fundamental principle of "free flow of information" enshrined in its constitution.

International Freedom of Expression Exchange Network (IFEX)

This was launched by several NGO's concerned with more effective pooling of information. IFEX set up an electronic alert and co-ordination network to react whenever freedom of information is threatened. Since September 1992, the network is run in Toronto, by the Canadian committee to protect Journalists, with the support of the UNESCO and its International Programme for the Development of Communication (IPDC). The IFEX network including major organizations as its members. IFEX set up a veritable system of alert a solidarity among all the protagonists. A data bank has been created on the Internet, which makes available the information gathered by IFEX on a world wide web server (www.IFEX.org).

Current Awareness Service (CAS)

Information is now being generated at such a tremendous rate, that is why its communication with out loss of time has become a serious problem. The gap in time from the generation of information and its announcement is increasing. To solve this problem and to reduce the time gap, a new service has emerged. Through this service, the newly generated information brought to users in the shortest time, possible is known as Current Awareness Service-CAS.

Characteristics of CAS (Current Awareness Service)

CAS notifies/announces title or abstracts of documents as soon as they appear. This response is not in response to a particular enquiry.

- CAS is that dissemination service which is intended to keep a user abreast with the latest information or development in his field of interest. It is an announcement service to satisfy the current approach to information.
- This service is not in response to a particular enquiry but a continuous process of keeping the users abreast with the latest information. It gives a panoramic view of the current developments in their field work and also in the related fields.
- The coverage of a CAS will always be broader than the specific/limited subject area of the users. This provides him an opportunity to know about other related subject areas in addition to his own.
- Speed/timeliness is the soul of CAS. Its aim is to notify the information to the users as quickly as possible.
- A CAS supplements the information which a user receives

from his own informal channels. This formal service makes up for what he misses in the informal channels.

- A CAS usually easy to use and such no search strategy is needed for its consultation.
- A CAS is for temporary use. Its contents are absorbed by indexing and abstracting journals after some time.

Forms and Formats of CAS

- Journals
- Reports
- Conference Proceedings
- Research Abstracts

Selective Dissemination of Information (SDI)

SDI – A History

In late 1950's Hans Peter Luhn of the IBM gave the concept of SDI to the world for the first time. Luhn was of the view that the areas of interest of modern scientists and engineers have long ceased to conform to the conventional concepts of disciplines. To meet this situation, he felt that there was a need of an information system which should monitor incoming documents to find out which one could satisfy the needs of a particular user, so that the user might be informed about the availability of that document.

In 1958, Luhn conceived an information system for this purpose. Based on his design, a full-fledged mechanized system was introduced by the,

IBM in 1959. It was named as SDI-I.

Later on more important systems, such as, SDI-2, SDI-3, SDI-4, SDI-5.

Were developed and implemented. Today SDI is considered as the most important information service.

The development and acceptance of SDI has been quite rapid. The factors made it possible,

- Availability of computer facilities at an increased rate.
- Application of computer in type setting, which helps in generating almost automatically a machine-readable data base.
- The vast expansion of world literature which makes it more difficult and expensive to keep abreast with all the relevant literature.

- The new advancements like Internet and availability of Internet editions of libraries, books, Journals, etc.

Selective Dissemination of Information (SDI)-Definition

"Any procedure whether manual or automated that attempts to provide a personalized current awareness service, selecting for each individual served, the current literature of probable relevance to his research interest may be considered as a SDI system" Connor J.H.

SDI-Characteristics

- It is a current awareness service meant to keep its user abreast with the latest development in the field of his interest.
- It is a personalized service meant for an individual or a group of users have identical information needs.
- Information provided through SDL is exactly tailored meet the specific informations needs of each user.
- It is quick service which provides pin-pointed information.
- It is meant for the specialists and research workers.

Comparison of SDI and CAS

- Both SDI and CAS are intended to keep a seeker of Information abreast with the latest development in his field of interest.
- SDI is a current awareness service with a very important difference.
- SDI meant for an individual and is restricted exclusively to the area of interest.
- In SDI what is not required by the user is not served to him.
- The principle on which SDI is based is that no two users have identical information needs.
- In SDI each one should be provided with only that information that is actually needed.
- SDI is user oriented.
- SDI saves the effort of searching on the part of the user by directly presenting him the information he needs. In CAS it requires some effort on the part of user to locate information.
- CAS is not in response to a particular enquiry, and is meant for a group of users.
- CAS is an all embracing information service.
- CAS is a general appetizer.

- CAS users with divergent information needs are served by the same documentation list and it is for each one of them to find out that information which is relevant to his needs.

MODEL QUESTIONS

1. "Computers together with internet become a mass media." Justify.
2. Why is computer education very important?
3. Briefly describe various aspects of education in which ICT can be used to advantage.
4. Differentiate CAS and SDI.
5. What is the need of regulations on medias? Why it different from to one country to another?
6. What are the bases of the progress and changes in ICT?
7. What are changes made by ICT in journalism/media sector?

REFERENCES

1. Alan Han Cock, *Planning for Educational Mass Media.* London: Longman.
2. Emery: Edwin *et. al.* (1987). *Introduction to Mass Communication.* Vakil, Preffer and Simens (Pvt.).
3. Malhan, P.N. (1985). *Communication Media Yesterday, Today & Tomorrow.* Ministry of Information and Broadcasting. New Delhi: Government of India.
4. Mcqual, D. (1987). *Mass Communication Theory.* Sage Publication.
5. U.K. Singh and K.N. Sudarshan, *Media Education.*

4

New Information Technology in Education

New Information Technology and its Functions

Information technology deals with all the information activities. It is concerned with computing, micro-electronic and telecommunication equipments which make the location, processing and transfer of information feasible in the shortest possible time. The new IT is overtaking the old, providing more and powerful ways to create, store, process, deliver and display information. New IT is new technology applied to the creation, storage, selection, transformation and distribution of various kinds of information. New IT depends less on mechanical means. Instead, its machines are electronic. New IT depends on computing, micro-electronics and telecommunications. Today these complex technologies are converging together.

Functions of New Information Technology

1. Making Information

- Making information is sub-divided into creating, collecting, selecting and transforming.
- Creating information is the first step in making information. Collecting information means bringing together information from many sources.
- Selecting Information precedes and follows collecting. This consists discrimination of information from massive information.
- Transforming information means re-arranging, re-ordering and preparing the collected/selected information for presentation.

2. Sending/ Receiving Information

New IT enhances the efficiency of transmission/sending/receiving of information.

3. Storing Information

New IT can convert information into the most economical form. We are using variety of storage devices today.

4. Displaying Information

Display may be on a screen or on a paper, or soft or Hard (Print) mode.

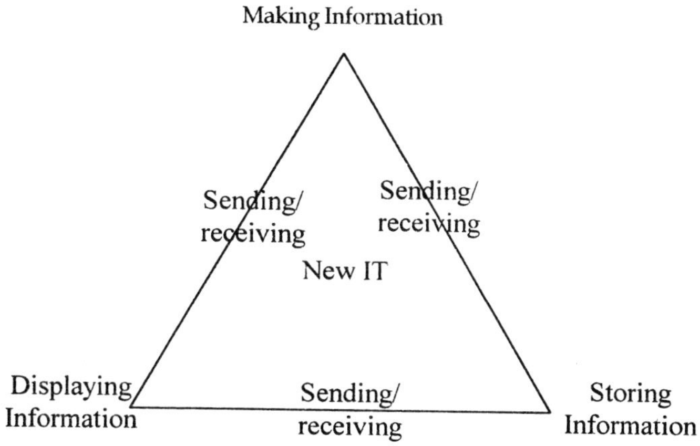

Integration of all these functions is made possible by new IT by combining them.

New IT for Learning at Home and Pre-Schools

New IT is used in education-formal, informal and non-formal, at all levels. Very young children itself are today operating TV sets, audio/ video players and such kind of electronic IT equipments. In the home today every one is accessing world wide IT channels via cable network and DTH's (Direct to Home). Some channels offer interactive facilities and educational games/programmes. 'Intelligent toys' functioning with the elements of IT are also useful at this stage. Children who learn Information and Communication Technology (ICT) is to be high achievers at both home and school.

IT in Primary Schools

Today most of the primary schools function with IT facilities. This help the students to acquire IT skills and computer literacy.

To acquire computer literacy, children must learn by actual experiences. Playing games and using softwares like 'MS Paint' helping them to acquire 'Key board literacy' and 'mouse movements' and casually they learn how to operate the various components.

Familiarizing with new IT in primary classes can serve the following utility functions.

(i) Logic games can be used to practice problem solving.

(ii) For learning languages i.e., they are motivated to read the ocroon.

(iii) Use of printers helping them in writing, editing and publishing. For example, releasing class newspaper, project works, etc.

(iv) For using Video/Audio CD's for educational purpose, that helps to learn subject effectively.

IT in Secondary Schools

During this stage the level of IT learning has increased. During this level,

- Hardware and Software training can be started.
- IT studied as a separate discipline.
- Chances to students to work with computer based projects.
- Programmes for the improvement of literature.
- Computers used to simulate experiments in science and geography.
- Use of IT to provide interactive learning via multimedia and internet.
- Use of IT for measurement and evaluation.

IT in Teacher Education

Many of the Indian universities recently introduced IT as a core part of the pre-service teacher education programmes. Central and State Governments today make efforts to train IT skills to their teachers in service. These efforts help the teachers to address the issue of 'digital divide' in a holistic manner. Government of Kerala created many programmes to impart ICT skills among all teachers of both school and colleges. Quality Improvement Programmes (QIP's) will be conducted for staff of educational institutions with the co-operation and involvement of professional organizations. Eventhough the above said efforts and initiations from the side of government, a minority of teachers in service perceive this in a doubtful way.

The present teacher training programmes covers,

- Computer studies i.e., computer as an instrument.
- Computer assisted/managed learning.
- Information technology.

Inservice IT training consisting of three levels,

1. Awareness level (1-3 days courses)
2. Expertise level (½ weeks to understand mastery skills)
3. Advanced level/Top level (upto 3 months).

IT in Higher Education

IT courseware at higher education level is improving in quality and variety. Teachers in higher education freely allow students to use the technology of learning. Funds, financial provisions for hardware, software, amenities are more readily available at this level. University libraries are pioneers in using New ICT to assist teachers, students, researchers, and scholars.

Eg: INFLIBNET- Information Library Network
OCLC-Online Computer Library Centres

These facilities provide libraries with a sharing acquisition and cataloguing service. OCLC uses computerized information databases for its functioning. Today most of the universities offering internet usage free of cost or with a nominal fee. It helps the learning community to access internet editions of books, journals, and educational data bases. It also make online consultation/E-mail with experts/resource persons.

IT in Vocational and Continuing Education

Vocational and continuing education agencies are already taking advantage of new IT to provide services to learners.

The following advancements in the field of IT are helpful for vocational and continuing education.

1. Simulation and Interactive Video Disc

Vocational training/situations/activities etc. are able to demonstrate with the help of computer, video disk, etc. The situation/activity/training divided into different segments. The segments covers visual cues, instruments, and the approach.

Video discs, video cassettes, cable, open circuit television are etc. also used in this field.

IT for Non/Informal Learning for Adults

Adults use new IT for their education nonformally. It doesn't depend on government funding. Adults can learn non-formally in computers from their own homes. Adults gain computer literacy with the help of their computer. With some assistance they can also learn mastery level. Adults also achieve learning through interactive video disc, cable television, network television etc.

Variety of Learning Sources of Non/Informal are;

- News services
- Electronic mail system
- Message system
- Data base search services
- Health and medicine information
- Personal financial information services
- Travel leisure pursuits information
- Buying service and
- Games and educational services.

Computers for Testing and Monitoring

This involves setting up some means for storing a set of questions in the computer and then specifying the rules which the machine can follow to make up a test from the available questions.

The computer can help to construct a number of different tests with the same characteristics. This facility helps for

- re-testing and
- giving equivalent tests to all.

Steps of Computerized Test Construction

1. Item Banking

The first task is to build up a file of question, called Item Banking, by using DBMS.

The all formalities of achievement test construction are following here too.

2. Test Construction

It may be done in a automated or in a printed manner.

3. Item Analysis

4. Scoring/Test Marking

Role of the Teacher

Traditionally, there is an assumption that the teacher should be the only and authoritative source of information. Today information is not the monopoly of the teacher.

Today new IT offer an increased access to a variety of rich information sources. Teacher should be able to compete with the entertainment industry concerning the presentation of information.

Today, a balance of control among teachers and students needs a shift, from 'vertical' to 'horizontal'.

Both students and teachers will have to accept that. They have a joint responsibility, for the goals and methods of learning.

Many teachers may feel uncomfortable in taking up new roles and tasks because they consider it as a threat to their control and authority.

Some of the teachers feel that many students know more about ICT than their teachers. This feeling leads to an inferiority complex. But in real, sense the roles and tasks of teachers are still vital and ICT add value to learning. Similarly teachers will have to develop their expertise in promoting. Students to search for information, access, evaluate and synthesize information.

MODEL QUESTIONS

1. What are the functions of new IT?
2. List and briefly describe various aspects of education in which ICT can be used to advantage.
3. Describe the role of games and computer stimulations in teaching and learning.
4. Can new ICT replace the teacher? Give arguments in support of your answer.

REFERENCE

Prasad, K. (Ed.) (2004). *Information and Communication Technology: Recasting Development*. Delhi: B.R. Publishing Corporation.

5
Education Via Internet

Internet

The internet is a world wide communication system. That is often referred as the Net or the Information Super Highway. Although it was initially used for military and academic purposes. It later graduated into a business tool.

According to surveys in 2005 there are more than sixty million users connected to the services of internet. Internet has a long history. It has its roots in US Military and Pentagon.

The History of Internet

After the Soviet Launch of 'Sputnik' satellite in 1957, the US Military established the Advanced Research Projects Agency (ARPA). Later renamed Defense Advanced Research Project Agency (DARPA) to fund research in areas of potential benefit to the military. As a result of this research, a network known as the ARPANET was set up in 1969, laying the foundation for the present internet.

During 1960 many different computer networks began to emerge. They are small in size and they used their own set of PROTOCOLS- to communicate each other. Since each network had its own protocols it was impossible for two different networks to communicate with each other.

By late 1973 DARPA come out with a new protocol suite called, the Transmission Control Protocol/Internet Protocol (TCP/IP).

The adoption of TCP/IP in 1975 connected a hundred more small networks with their inter-netting project. In 1984 all the military information was removed from the ARPANET and in 1985 the

National Science Foundation (NSF) of USA took over its control. They called it NSFNET and linked several computers from famous universities. During late 1980's the numbers of internet users and network constituents expanded internationally and started commercial facilities.

World Wide Web

The www incorporates all the internet services and much more. The www (web) contain different kinds of material such as text, graphics, video, formatted documents, pictures, multi-player games, movies, files, programmes for downloading, audio, animation, etc. It also offers the facility to chat. Some of these applications involve quick data transfer. The www was introduced by Tim-Berners Lee. www considered as one of the key mite stones of Internet usage.

A new development of www which is set to change our lives is electronic commerce/E-commerce. The new state of art techniques are converting websites into virtual shopping malls.

Why People Use the Internet?

- To find general information about a subject.

For example, www.britanica.com

- To access information not easily available elsewhere.
- To meet people i.e., the facilities like matrimonial websites, Blog etc.
- To correspond with far away friends via E-mail.
- To discuss their interests with like minded people.

For example, www.barefooters.org

- To have fun, for example, www.kissthisguy.com
- To learn – online education
- To read news- www.timesofindia.com
- To find software - www.shareware.com
- To buy things - www.amazon.com

Why Do People Put Things on the Web

- To advertise a product – for example www.adobe.com
- To sell a product
- To make money

The Altavista search engine at www.altavista.com is an example of a site that makes money from banner advertisement.

Services on the Internet

The services available on the internet can be broadly classified, into two:

- Communication Services
- Information Retrieval Services

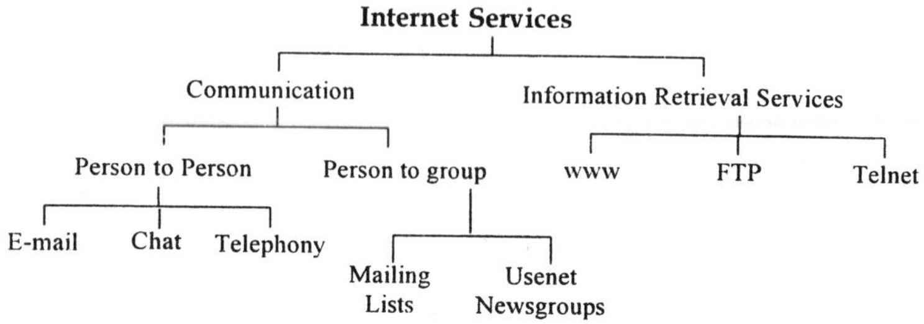

Electronic Mail (E-mail)

E-mail is an application in which any user on a network can send/ receive letters/attached files/pictures, video on his computer terminal to/from any person in the world who has an electronic mail address.

Mail can be sent not only to individuals but to groups, by using group identity. In 1971 an Engineer Ray Tomlinson sent the first E-mail.

File Transfer Protocol (FTP)

Mail is intended for short messages. FTP is the ability to rapidly transfer entire files from one computer to another, intact, for viewing or other purposes.

Downloading and Uploading are the processes of transferring files to and from a computer. If you get something from a remote computer, it is called down loading, and if you send something to a computer. It is referred to as uploading.

Telnet/Remote Login

It is an internet service that allows one computer to log on to another.

Eg: for using the book index of American library of congress, you type telnet locis-loc.gov.

Usenet (User's Network)

It allows you to post articles and messages to facilitate online discussions in thousands of e-mail groups and news-groups, where related topics are discussed.

If you have question, all that you have to do is post the question in the appropriate group and you are assured of getting a reply from someone.

A software that runs on each PC to make usenet possible is called a *Newsreader*.

Internet Education

Why Use the Internet in Education

There are many advantages to using the services of the Internet, particularly the tools and resources on the web, in Education.

- Instruction materials such as syllabi, lecture notes, presentations, assignments and announcements could be made available online.
- The internet puts the concept of "any time, any where" into a higher level as far as learning is concerned.
- Students will be able to learn at their pace. The primary beneficiaries would be students and adult learners who are too far or too busy to attend classes. Even traditional/regular students will benefit when instructional materials are available to support or complement classroom attendance.
- Students will be able to prepare for the next class if they are reminded of the assignments and topics of discussion.
- Those who missed classes or missed the teachers point can go over the lecture notes and presentation.
- Both teacher and student will also benefit from being able to research any topic from library catalogs, topical data bases, and the www.
- Anonymous FTP and Telnet will allow them to access public data bases maintained by Government Institutions.
- Services like e-mail and mailing lists can support communication between teacher and student, and among peers. (Teacher to teacher, student to student).

Using a combination of e-mail and the web, teachers and students can collaborate on research and creative projects even with those who don't live in the same city or country.

The variety of information resources available in many educational websites is also growing.

With streaming audio and video, students can now look over archeologists shoulders as they dig for may an artifacts in South America, observe animals in the zoo, interact with astronauts at NASA all in real time.

The multimedia and interactive capabilities of the internet and web will make active learners out of students. The virtual learning environment can be re-inforced by MUD's (Multi-User Dimension) where students can engage one another in adventure games that demand problem-solving skills and good imagination.

Functions Served by Internet

Hypermedia—Audio-visual information conceptually linked with other data types on the web.

Interactive Multimedia—In the place of the text only web pages the internet now offers sound, video, and animation.

Distribution of Information—The information (text/graphics) can be successfully delivered over the internet.

Dissemination of Information—Internet today is a means of disseminating information and facilitating learning. Search engines are good Selective Dissemination of Information (SDI) tools.

Need Based Instruction

Unlike TV networks computer networks are invariably 2-way. TV networks send the same information to all the stations at the same time; in the computer networks, each particular message is usually routed to a particular computer.

E-mail

Electronic mail, another important, popular and widely using internet facility.

Surfing/Browsing/Navigation

Surfing the net means checking out sites on the web. The software used to navigate the web is known as a browser.

For example, Microsoft Internet Explorer
Netscape Navigator
Crazy Browser
Mozilla Fire Fox, etc.

Search Engines

Search engines are special tools that help to search information on the Net

For example, Yahoo-www.yahoo.com
Google-www.google.com
Altavista-www.altavista.com
Hot Bot-www.hotbot.com

Search engines keep track of information available on the internet.

E-Commerce – It is the word for buying and selling stuff over the net via using credit cards.

Internet education is the need of today and achieving it will increase efficiency, effectiveness and competitiveness.

Distance Education Via Internet

Today many Indian and western universities offering courses via online.

For example, Belfrod University, United Kingdom
Kilban University, USA
Anna University, Tamil Nadu etc.

In 1997 James Madison University firstly started a remote distance master programme. The programme is almost lecture less. The instructors meet the students only twice-during the course. Firstly in an initial stage and in final to 'wrap up' the course. The remaining 'sessions' of the programme via internet and e-mail, telephone, fax or by any other means.

The student access all the information through the website. The instructor clarifies any point that has reached a plateau or trouble.

The statistical results indicates that there is no significant differences between the 'on-campus' and 'off-campus' students.

Interactive Distance Learning Over the Internet

Interactive distance learning provides learning through interaction from a remote distance. This involve two major efforts.

- The implementation of computer based-training activities meant to provide learning guidance, to supply detailed data for analysis.
- The implementation of distance learning technology to link the Small Group Instructors (SGIs).

Initially the students attend large group instruction together. Then the students disperse into groups.

A Small Group Instructor (SGI) is assigned to each group. The small group is required to involve in the decision making process to analyze tools detailed in the text.

In total there are four phases.

1. Analysis
2. Course of Action (COA) development
3. COA analysis and comparison
4. Execution.

The primary role of the instructor is to facilitate the tactical decision making process, as students try to formulate effective Courses of Action (COA's).

The instructor will review, score and provide feed back to the group for each submitted product. These products are used to measure of student achievement.

The interactive distance learning is applicable and adoptable to hearing impaired/mentally retarded/speech disordered persons via written texts/pictures, symbols etc. That means interactive distance learning provides an Augmentative and Alternative Communication (AAC).

Interactive Multimedia

Interactive multimedia technology is the computer delivered electronic system that allows the user to control, combine, and manipulate different types of media such as, text, sound, video, graphics and animation. For example, online teaching/training, medical transcription, tutorial CD's, etc.

The user is required to activate, manipulate and respond to the presentation of instructional material and to control the rate and the route taken through the interactive instructional module.

Advantages

Multimedia systems are very effective for training and education, due to:

1. Multi-sensory communication.
2. The huge quantity of learning material which can be integrated in them.
3. Synchronization of motion, text, visuals.
4. The access facilities to the learning material.

Benefits

- Interactive and dynamic learning in the place of passive learning
- It gives the option to personalize the style of studying
- Make study more appropriate and effective

Desk Top Video Conferencing

Desk top video conferencing is an Educational Strategy that uses Computer Mediated Communication (CMC) to combine distance education and face-to-face instruction.

Desk top video conferencing offers on-line courses, many-to-many communication through Computer Mediated Communication (CMC) techniques.

Computer mediated communication happens in four ways:

1. Information retrieval or one-alone technique
   This primarily focus on the development of 'self-directed learning'. The learner himself taking the initiative regarding.
2. E-mail or one-to-one technique
   One to one technique uses E-mail for learner-to-learner and learner-instructor interaction.
3. Bulletin boards or one-to-many techniques
   It is one-to-many text based techniques. For example, News groups, Banners in the web pages.
   These techniques are casual in nature and free of rigid time constraints.
4. Computer Conferencing or Many-to-Many Technique
   This includes project groups, video conferencing, and audio conferencing.

Interactive Technical Documentation

Paper based documentation is a himalayan task in the present world of knowledge explosion. Many institutions are trying to find alternatives to eliminating these difficulties.

Interactive Technical Documentation allow to access large amounts of textual and visual data in an associative way.

Multimedia presentations/programmes are now effectively used in the Interactive Technical Documentation because it allows;

- Electronic exchange of technical information

- Presenting and searching for information contained in the instructional manuals.

Computer Literacy Courses

Computer Literacy Mission Society of India

Computer Literacy Mission Society of India is a non-profit educational organization working autonomously for Computer Literacy Mission of Government of India. It's Head Quarter at Chandigarh. It working for the promotion of computer and IT education in India and reaching the masses with its affordable training forums. It's mission is that, "Serve the ambitions."

Objectives

- To create a genuine platform to ensure quality computer education and software training to the large community and masses.
- To increase IT awareness and PC penetration to Indian society by various campaigns.
- To hold computer awareness seminars and centralized IT camps in remote areas.
- To provide professional courses and university degrees for students on nominal and affordable cost.
- To arrange the financial support and scholarships to deserving students in association with financial institutions.
- Welfare and educational activities for the public.

Institutions with Computer Literacy Mission Society of India

1. Centre for System Software Technologies (CSST)

CSST's offering High-Tech courses in system programming, system integration, office automation, Network management etc. on the various parts of India through the franchesies.

2. Institute of Information Technology and Engineering (IITE)

IITE launched university degree programmes like MCA, M.Tech, M.Sc, BCA, B.Tech and PG Diplomas duly awarded by the university. IITE is the authorized centres for the above courses and forms a mini-engineering college.

Supporting Organizations

- BCMT Computer Centre
- Innovative Computer Helpline

- Jaan Group of Companies
- Jaan Net Link Inc. USA
- Jet Age Application Netlink (P) Ltd.

Rajiv Gandhi Computer Literacy Programme (RGCLP)

RGCLP launched by Government of Assam to impart computer education in the Higher Secondary Classes of the state at free of cost.

Assam State Planning and Development Department and AMTRON (The State Nodel Agency for IT) tie up with NIIT & CMC for this project.

The first phase of RGCLP covering 200 schools was launched on 19th February 2004. Phase IV launched on 11th February 2006.

RGCLP at a Glance

- Covering all Higher Secondary Schools of the Assam.
- Classes covered V-XII.
- Linux based curriculum.
- Students no need to pay fees.
- Computer aided education on four subjects viz., English, Mathematics, Social Science and General Science.
- Testing and certification at the end of every academic year.

ERNET-Education and Research Network

ERNET is a joint effort of Department of Electronics of Government of India and United Nation's Development Programme (UNDP).

The objective of ERNET was to create expertise in Research, Development (R&D) and Education in the areas of networking and internet in the country.

ERNET, one of the largest nationwide terrestrial and satellite network today. Research, development and training are integral parts of ERNET.

Mission of ERNET

Benefit education and research institutions—through innovation, quality, productivity, human development and growth- away striving for excellence within the frame work of the madate of Ministry of Information Technology.

ERNET offering quality service to the educational institutions and programmes through innovation, speed, flexibility and service of empowered employees.

MODEL QUESTIONS

1. List the uses of the internet in education.
2. What are the various ways in which the internet could be utilized in distance education?
3. What are search engines? Give any two examples.
4. IT and multimedia replace the teacher? Give arguments in support of your answer.
5. Through a brain storming session how do you give awareness among your students about the indiscriminate use of internet?
6. What is ERNET?
7. What is Internet? How will you utilize Internet in education?

REFERENCES

1. Das, S.K. (2005). *A Text Book of Information Technology*. New Delhi: Dominant Publishers and Distributors.
2. Ratnajeevan, S. *et al.* (2005). *ICT for Teachers*. New Delhi: Foundation Books.
3. Sethumadhavan, P. *Internet Oru Padanam* (Malayalam). Calicut: Lipi Publications.
4. www.mission_india.org

6
Role of Electronic Media in Education

ROLE OF MEDIA

Enrichment of Instruction

In the formal education system individualization of instruction and optimum utilization of teachers capabilities is a major problem. How to make the best use of a teacher, so that he can attend to the needs of an individual student and at the same time his expertise is available to the largest number of students? The formal education system imparts some basic knowledge (consisting of concepts, principles and procedures), basic skills (both physical and verbal), and basic attitudes to function effectively within a given working environment. In the present formal education system the teacher gives a lot of stress on verbal instruction by using lecture as the predominant way of imparting instruction. In order to make instruction more meaningful, students also need both enactive as well as iconic experiences in addition to the symbolic presentation of information through lectures. Enactive experiences are gained through actual participation of the learner in learning events. If it is difficult by providing direct access to such experience, the learner at least provide the opportunity to understand the actual sequence of events. This is possible through motion-film and video tapes. Iconic experience is presented through pictures or graphics which represent real world through models. This is made possible through video displays. Presentation of enactive and iconic experiences in the classroom requires the use of motion films and video displays.

Effective presentation of graphics for providing iconic experience can do only with the help of projection media and video display.

This media can also be used advantageously for explaining those basic concepts particularly which cannot be demonstrated in real life. For example the movement of atomic and sub-atomic particles, and working of biological cells. Enactive and iconic experiences are also needed in order to change the attitude of students. For developing positive attitudes in inter-personal relations, sympathy for the poor and disadvantaged sections of society, respect for honesty, passion for quality and justice, needs simulation techniques, case study techniques, or bringing into the classroom examples of model behaviour. These are some of the gaps in conventional instruction which are rectified through technological aids with great success.

Educational psychologists emphasize that in order to achieve specific educational objectives every student needs different types of educational experiences depending on his entry behaviour. The teacher, therefore, should produce/acquire, and organize variety of resources and use them in the classroom to suit individual's learning needs.

It is also now recognized that mere provision of information through lectures does not suffice to equip students with some critically important skills like the ability to analyze one's environment, develop solutions on one's own, and communicate effectively. A student can learn these only when he is motivated to set his own learning goals, chooses his own learning experiences and is allowed to learn at his own pace; all of which are integral part of independent study skill. Technological aids can be used to strengthen independent study skills among learners.

Increasing Effectiveness of Lecturing

The presentation can be enriched by using multimedia information and resources. Now-a-days, lectures are supplemented by tape recordings, filmstrips, set of slides and transparencies, OHP transparencies, etc. With the advent of video and computer, real-life events can be brought into the classroom through video-films. It is also possible to supplement the lecture by bringing the best available presentation in a particular subject into the classroom. Computer has made the use of animation and simulation techniques much easier and thereby helped the teacher in explaining complex concepts.

Increasing Effectiveness of Laboratory Instruction

The student-teacher ratio in a normal laboratory class varies between 10:1 and 15:1. This is because the operation and demonstration of the laboratory experiments by the teacher cannot be done effectively to a large class. Secondly, intermittent individual guidance by the teacher during the course of experimentation also requires a smaller student to staff ratio. The need for teacher involvement can be reduced somewhat by the use of self-instructional print material. But print material alone is not capable of reducing the load of the teacher or to ensure individual guidance. It is now possible to prepare 8 mm films or video-tapes to explain the total sequence of laboratory experimentation including explanation of procedure, and thereby permit the teacher to help larger number of students. Furthermore, stimulation plays a very important part where discovery learning is the objective of laboratory instruction i.e., where students are expected to discover for themselves certain principles and laws through laboratory experiments. In this computers can play an important part by allowing quick and extensive exploration of the simulated experimental system.

Increasing Effectiveness of Independent Study

Independent study in the institution as well as at home is normally done with the help of print materials. Its effectiveness can be greatly increased if additional experiences can be provided through non-print media and the student is in a position to access a variety of experiences and information. For example, he should be able to listen to the lecture of an expert, retrieve textual and pictorial information from motion films or any other source, and process information. This a possible if he is supported with television set, VCRs, micro computers, film projectors, radios, etc.

Increasing Reach of the Teacher

Since teacher is the costliest resource in any educational venture, it is necessary to ensure that the teacher is accessible to as many students as possible without affecting the individual needs of the students. In USA it has been shown that with the help of interactive television a professor can successfully teach 200-300 students at a time. The difficulties of student-teacher interaction due to larger number can be overcome by electronically operated feedback system.

Establishment of Resource Centre

In its traditional concept a library is a place where only print material are stored for use by students and teachers. There is a need to extend the scope of library to production, acquisition and storing non-print information resources as well. In modern terms a library which stores a variety of information resources is a Resource Centre. A typical Resource Centre uses micro-film and micro-fiche for storing large amounts of documented information thus reducing requirement of storage space. It provides space for hardware needed for projecting retrieving, and recording information. The resources centre also stores, in addition to text-books, a variety of other print material like monographs, Journals, Articles, Newspaper clippings etc. It also stores audio cassettes, video cassettes, films transparencies, and slides. But storage and retrieval through these information resources are being managed at the moment, largely manually which is too inefficient, and slow. With increase in the use and variety of A.V. aids in course of time, electronically operated system of information storage and retrieval will have to be introduced.

MODEL QUESTIONS

1. How media enriching classroom instruction?
2. How media increasing the effectiveness of Lecturing?

REFERENCE

Pathak, G.P. (2005). Education and Communication Technology. New Delhi: Reference Press.

7
Issues of Technology in Education

'The Digital Divide'

The use of educational technology is significantly altering access to higher education. New technologies are lessening geographical barriers to education. Individuals and institutions with access to the internet have an enormous volume of educational materials at their disposal, regardless of their physical location. However, such access comes at a price, and the need for expensive hardware, software and telecommunications poses a serious financial barrier for much of the population of the region.

Academics in poor countries such as Vietnam are beginning to obtain internet access, which allows them to keep up to date with international developments in the field, access publications and maintain international networks of colleagues. This requirement is increasing infrastructure costs for educational institutions, which is particularly difficult for public institutions in poor countries. This also creates new barriers to entry for prospective students, who are increasingly required to have independent access to computer equipment and internet access. The geographical centre-periphery divide in education is slowly being replaced by a digital divide between those who can afford to participate in global information networks and those who cannot.

The use of information and communication technologies in education is expanding access to information, educational products and whole courses, which are coming to form a globalised information network. Access to these technologies is a precondition for participation in a global information society. Clearly, individuals and institutions that are able to access and participated in these global networks are at an advantage. However, there are, of course, huge disparities in access to information and communications technologies. In recent years, inequalities in access to new information and communications technologies have become increasingly apparent.

On a global scale, the cosmopolitanism of the wealthy is in stark contrast to the localism of the poor. With economic globalization, increasingly the wealthy have ready access to global communications media, work for companies with branches in many countries, have colleagues and clients from different cultural backgrounds, travel regularly for business and pleasure, and generally think, feel and act transnationally (Castells, 1989). The groups which are 'information rich' in the sense that they have ready access to information and communications technology, also possess a worldview that is disembedded enough from the particularities of local conditions to allow them to traverse the cultural differences of a global arena with relative ease. In wealthier societies, such as Australia the United States and Singapore, a large proportion of the population have access to such networks. Public education systems in these countries are connected to global flows of information, albeit with inferior machines and lower bandwidth than the private education sector. In poorer countries, much smaller segments of the popular are able to participate. Public education systems are stretched providing more basic services across the country, while private education institutions offer those who can afford it an entry point into the global information society.

'Virtual Universities'

The term 'virtual university' is usually reserved for institutions that have no campus and teach students exclusively by distance mode using educational technologies. This is perhaps the most intensive application of educational technologies into higher education, evidenced in the United States by universities such as Jones International University. In a technical sense, relying on Internet-based communication allows the institution to operate globally. In the earlier print/post phase of remotely-supported distance education, most students tended to live near the institution, and almost entirely within the same country. Internationalization was difficult due to the cost, slowness and unreliability of international communications. By using e-mail and the Web, it is now possible for prospective students to choose from a wide range of courses offered by providers based in many different nations. However, in practice, online universities appear to draw most of their students from within their home country. A number of online universities have begun to market themselves internationally, including Jones International and the University of Southern Queensland.

University Tun Abdul Razak (UNITAR) is a private university in Malaysia founded in 1998 that set out to be 'virtual' university with no physical campus, relying entirely on technologically-mediated communications.

When the university was first proposed, the Malaysia Education Minister expressed concern about the lack of socialization in remotely-supported distance education. In short, UNITAR was told: 'no socialization, no education, no license, no operation'. In response, the virtual university model was altered, requiring compulsory attendance at local study centres in all subjects. In the first semester, attendance is required for 22 hours per subject and in subsequent semesters students must attend eight hours of classes per subject. UNITAR has had to establish a network of local learning centres, which students can attend for classes, interaction, exams and access to computers and support. These are very similar to the learning centres of established distance education providers, but with more reliance on educational technologies.

Due to the cost and unreliability of dial-up Internet connections in Malaysia, which were then prone to drop-outs and low bandwidth, UNITAR decided to distribute teaching materials to students on CD-ROMs. Students are required to go online to access the library, complete administrative tasks, participate in forums and tutorials. UNITAR established a courseware team consisting of 120 instructional designers, multimedia programmers, graphic designers and audio-visual producers. They work with lecturers and module writers, most of whom are employed on contract.

UNITAR's online content is primarily text-based, including answers to common questions from students, which are compiled into a FAQ (Frequently Asked Questions) list. Threaded discussion forums display only the last week's messages, encouraging students to read and respond regularly. Virtual tutorials are held once or twice each month, using chat, a shared whiteboard and Real Audio.

UNITAR has a virtual library which holds 3,000 titles, mainly online journals. UNITAR responds to students requests and complaints through a call centre. This forwards queries on to the appropriate person by e-mail, and they should respond within 24 hours.

TMC is part owner of a Singapore-based online education company, CyberCampus 21, which hosts online courses and provides related technical and educational services. These services include providing hardware, software and support services to both educational providers and users. CyberCampus 21 currently offers an online course that is taught by TMC and a Diploma in Business Administration and Marketing that is validated by Staffordshire University on a pilot run basis. They also offer two short courses called Servesafe Food Safety Programme Writing Right: An Introductory Course to the Basics of Writing Well. TMC sees the online study option provided by CyberCampus 21 as one of a range of different delivery options, which their students can choose between. TMC plan to use CyberCampus 21 to offer a range of international courses in much the same way as they offer distance education courses. Online content would be provided by the International University and TMC would provide local marketing, administration, face-to-face teaching and student support.

These two institutions provide examples of two different types of 'virtual' university. UNITAR operates in a similar way to existing universities, developing and teaching its own courses, but the majority of its teaching and learning is done through computers. CyberCampus 21, by contrast, does not develop its own content but operates as a hosting service for the online components of distance education courses developed by other institutions.

While all the distance education providers visited in the course of this study were moving to incorporate educational technology, none were moving away from providing face-to-face teaching and support to students. There appeared to be no significant demand for remotely supported distance education. As in other parts of the world, online courses seem to be most popular with working adults seeking postgraduate qualifications, especially in business and information technology. For undergraduate students, the lack of on-campus socialization appears to be a significant disincentive.

MODEL QUESTIONS

1. Explain the concept 'Digital Divide'.
2. What you mean by virtual universities?

REFERENCE

Chandra, R. (2005). *Technology Integration in Education*. Delhi: Kalpaz Publications.

8
Teachers in a Changing World

The teachers are one of the largest group of trained professionals in the world. In everywhere good education requires good teachers. Teachers must learn to use the new information technologies and more and more will be expected of future teachers. Educational reforms intended to confront the challenges of the future must reach the educational establishment and the classroom. Awareness of this fact means that the teacher plays the key role in the future process of transforming education.

The experience of recent decades has confirmed that it is not possible to continue reforming education systems without taking the teachers into consideration; but, on the contrary, it was also confirmed that we cannot ask teachers to change without education itself changing. The success of educational policies depends to a great extent on the integrated nature of their training.

The regional discussions of the UNESCO's 45th session of the International Conference on Education (ICE) observed;

1. The professionalization of teaching activity is the best long-term strategy to improve the outcomes of education and, at the same time, the working conditions of teachers.
2. Pre-service and in-service training should be profoundly modified so as to enable teachers to gain mastery of the whole range of educational strategies adapted to the wide diversity of learning situations with which they will be confronted in carrying out their duties. This diversity and wide-range of situations can only be managed by teachers working as a team, and not as a isolated individual.

3. Teachers must learn to use the new information technologies.
4. Teachers will be appreciated not only for their knowledge and purely technical skills, but also for their personal qualities.

Today, teacher morale had gone down almost everywhere, standards have dropped and commitment is slowly being eroded away. The remedy is that, candidates entering teacher education programmes should be selected for their moral and intellectual suitability. During their training, teachers should also be introduced to research methods, as well as the use of computers.

In Indian context the rural-urban disparity is there. Many teachers work in rural communities, it was suggested that they should be offered special concessions in recognition of the difficulty facing them.

As custodians of education as a public good, the policy and resourcing of education rest ultimately with the governments, as does the direction of educational change in an evolving world. But the management of that change should involve teachers commitment to educational change.

It is necessary that, a legislation so as to render laws more appropriate to the multiple roles of teachers, and to grant them adequate autonomy making it easier for them to fulfil their new roles. The necessary measure should also be taken to involve teachers in planning and developing educational programmes.

The enormous potential represented by new information and communication technologies to improve education was recognized. Education systems must incorporate and learn to master them in order to avoid any subservience to technology, culture or economy, as well as any risk of the school being isolated to the fringes compared with other sections.

The report of the international commission on education for the twenty-first century remarked, "good education requires good teachers." In addition, in terms of their sheer numbers, teachers are very important. UNESCO's World Education Report (1995) indicates that throughout the world there are 53 million teachers in primary and secondary schools alone and this number will continue to increase.

Teachers and Social Change: Emerging Challenges

The world continues to experience constant change, there being unprecedented upheals in the socio-political and economic domains. Internationalization, globalization, knowledge explosion and technological advances are influencing all nations and regions of the world. In the light of such change, all countries are undertaking a critical re-assessment of their education systems. Education is seen as pivotal in dealing successfully with these changes, facilitating economic development, social cohesion, peace and tolerance.

Since the quality and effectiveness of any education system ultimately depends upon on the quality and effectiveness of teachers, one of the key issues which is attracting the attention of all countries is how best to accommodate the changing role and demands placed on teachers, which have implications for their recruitment, training, reward structure and the development of a new teacher profile.

New Information Technologies and Teachers

There is agreement from all regions that new information technologies have already began to or will provide a challenge of considerable importance to education systems, schools and teachers. It is important to identify aspects of this challenge interms of the impact already felt so that those who have not yet confronted this question may maximize the benefits and minimize the burdens.

One of the features of the advent of new information technologies are simply the size and diversity. Schools and teachers are now regarded as the sole repositories of knowledge. What will be their status in future? How can and will they be relevant? If these were not enough, there is the technology attending this information explosion, with its computers, language and skill demands.

New information technologies provide the means for changing the face of teaching both in systemic terms and in the localized setting of the school and classroom. New information technologies bring with them new subjects for the curriculum, such as computer education. Teachers and methods of teaching are forced to change with the advent of new information technologies. The streamlining of administrative processes to provide better means of both storing and networking information becomes very possible with the use of new technologies.

A very appealing application of new information technology in education is their application to distance education. This appeal arises from the large number of persons who can be accommodated at seemingly lower costs. The issue of the cost-effectiveness of distance education for teacher development requires more analysis.

Changing Demands

Teachers are confronted by a set of changes which lead to contradictory demands on them from society in short, that is,

- a commitment to Education For All (EFA).
- an extension of the period of initial schooling.
- recognition of the growing importance of life-long education.
- more emphasis on general education for children and young people which prepares them for life rather than providing vocational skills of specific jobs.
- increasing emphasis on team work and co-operation.
- a consensus that general education should include attention to the environmental issues, tolerance and mutual understanding.

In the conclusion concluding, there has been increasing recognition of the importance of the status of teachers. We note that the vast majority of teachers believe that they do not receive the moral and material recognition appropriate to their qualifications and responsibilities. UNESCO recommended that. "The status of teachers should be commensurated with the needs of education as assessed in the light of educational aims and objectives; It should be recognized that the proper status of teachers and due public regard for profession of teaching are of the major importance for the full realization of these aims and objectives."

MODEL QUESTIONS

1. How new information technologies influencing teaching and teachers?
2. Discuss the changing demands in teaching on the changing IT context?

REFERENCE

Rao, D.B. (Ed.) (2003). *Teachers in a Changing World*. New Delhi: Discovery Publishing House.

9

Information Technology and its Achievements

Information Technology (IT), as defined by the Information Technology Association of America (ITAA), is "the study, design, development, implementation, support or management of computer-based information systems, particularly software applications and computer hardware." IT deals with the use of electronic computers and computer software to convert, store, protect, process, transmit, and securely retrieve information.

Today, the term information technology has ballooned to encompass many aspects of computing and technology, and the term is more recognizable than ever before. The information technology umbrella can be quite large, covering many fields. IT professionals perform a variety of duties that range from installing applications to designing complex computer networks and information databases. A few of the duties that IT professionals perform may include data management, networking, engineering computer hardware, database and software design, as well as the management and administration of entire systems.

When computer and communication technologies are combined, the result is information technology, or "infotech." Information Technology (IT) is a general term that describes any technology that helps to produce, manipulate, store, communicate, and/or disseminate information. Presumably, when speaking of Information Technology (IT) as a whole, it is noted that the use of computers and informations are associated.

Information and Communication Technology – Or technologies (ICT) is an umbrella term that includes all technologies for the manipulation and communication of information. The term is sometimes used in preference to *Information Technology (IT)*, particularly in two communities: education and government. In the common usage it is often assumed that ICT is synonymous with IT; ICT in fact encompasses any medium to record information (magnetic disk/ tape, optical disks (CD/DVD), flash memory etc. and arguably also paper records); technology for broadcasting information—radio, television; and technology for communicating through voice and sounds or images—microphone, camera, loudspeaker, telephone to cellular phones. It includes the wide variety of computing hardware (PCs, servers, mainframes, network storage), the rapidly developing personal hardware market comprising mobile phones, personal devices, MP3 players, and much more; the full gamut of application software from the smallest home-developed spreadsheet to the largest enterprise packages and online software services; and the hardware and software needed to operate networks for transmission of information, again ranging from a home network to the largest global private networks operated by major commercial enterprises and, of course, the Internet. Thus, "ICT" makes more explicit that technologies such as broadcasting and wireless mobile telecommunications are included.

ICT capabilities vary widely from the sophistication of major western economies to lesser provision in the developing world. But the latter are catching up fast, often leapfrogging older generations of technology and developing new solutions that match their specific needs.

PC-based ICT

A PC (Personal Computer) connected to the Internet has become a vital tool for communicating, during the past few decades since its proliferation among the masses. However, while this mode of ICT has achieved much, it has its limitations in the context of the world at large.

Achievements

The Internet: The Internet has opened up many opportunities, from finding out information, conducting communications globally, e.g. through e-mail, voice mail, e-commerce or generally just having fun through on line chats or instant messaging. One often wonders: How did people manage before the time of the Internet? How much harder was it for people to communicate and find out information they need, quickly and easily? A PC connected to the Internet whether through a dial-up connection, broadband or Wi-Fi has indeed made it a facile act for many peoples.

Teaching -PC—Internet based ICT is currently used within the school curriculum. This kind of ICT is now seen as a core subject that is taught in some primary and secondary schools. The major advantage to this development is ICT has become a transferable subject. Computers or interactive whiteboards are now used across most school subjects as well as innovative schools using more technology like PDA's, Mobile (cell) phones and some game consoles. The interaction created by the use of this ICT makes lessons much more effective and allow children to learn in a way that they enjoy. Recent initiatives such as the One Laptop Per Child programme are contributing to this development.

Communications – Apart from Internet, a PC allows communication of information through Compact Discs, pen drives, printers, whether laser or inkjet, flash memory cards and exchange of information within a local network through LAN. As communications scholars Gasher and Lorimer articulated "We depend on technology for our communications with others-whether they are just a house or two away or halfway around the world. In the second half of the twentieth century it became almost impossible to live without a television in our homes, much less without a telephone, and now we can hardly live without personal computers through which we gain Internet access and send and receive e-mail. The reality of new communication technology is that anyone is able to get in touch with anyone else, anywhere, at any time, for very little money-at least in the developed world." (Gasher and Lorimer, Communications Technology and Society: Theory and Practice).

Work Related Aspects

As well as benefiting school students to gather information for assignments, PC based ICT is often used in other jobs such as in the police department, within libraries, in offices or even shops. It has also emerged as a source of employment in many emerging economies through Business process outsourcing or Knowledge process outsourcing from companies in the developed world. People now have the chance to conduct remote log on, in which they can access their work computers (For example in an office) from home. This has opened up many more opportunities for those that struggle to find time to leave their house to go to work, so they can now just work from home.

Limitations

Previous information communication technologies have penetrated deep into the society and hence are often very cost effective; teachers in developing countries often use no more than a blackboard and chalk to pass on information about any subject to the students. Printed papers in the form of books, magazines or newspapers have become a part of daily routine of any educated citizen, as are broadcast media such as radio and television. The photocopy machine is widely used by students to access information from books they cannot afford to buy. The cost of a PC connected to the Internet is often prohibitive in developing countries. Power needs, physical space and connectivity issues are also factors that add to the challenge of getting these technologies to take root in developing countries.

Limitations of PC-Internet Based ICT are

Bandwidth—The time taken to access a particular piece of information on the Internet depends on the bandwidth available to the user at that time. Often, it takes several minutes, using an economical connection, to download a piece of information. Thus a user may have to spend substantial time before he/she finds the information he/she seeks.

Language—At present most of the information available on the Internet is in English, a limiting factor at the very least.

Text/Voice—Most information on the Internet requires action by the user as opposed to the passive nature of television and radio. As most of the Internet's information is textual, the user must be able to read it. Even more passive forms of Internet information such as video-sharing Websites require action (and reading) by the viewer for navigation.

Disruptive Software—Internet users are often susceptible to computer viruses. Commercial anti-virus software is often prohibitively priced. Thin client technology is a small, but growing alternative.

Participation—Social networks and increased user-managed information stores have emerged in the early part of this century. Increased interaction between the content (whether it be delivered via Internet, television or radio) is leading to an information revolution.

Security—Internet safety is an issue that impacts every online user from small children to international corporations. When ABC went into public service broadcasting online in the early 1990s, the safety of their users was its top priority. The internet is an equalizer in that every user is vulnerable and in a sense, all at the same level. The emergence of weblogs, Internet forums and wikis is often grouped under the new technology umbrella term Web 2.0, and has helped to usher in a greater level of global participation.

Development

ICT can become a revolutionary vehicle in developing countries, provided technological innovations emerge on the following lines.

Local Content in Local Languages

The need of the hour is to enable the intelligentsia to develop information sources that are exclusively for fulfilling the needs of local communities. The content on the Internet that can fulfil these conditions is minuscule at present. Conditions have to emerge in which people are enthused to contribute towards the development of information databases that is exclusively disseminated through local networks, in languages/dialects that are popular in the region. The various modes of ICT may need to be integrated with one another, so that a meaningful volume of information can be generated in the minimum possible time.

Future

The ICT may not survive in its present form for long. Sooner than later developing countries would get over the PC mania prevalent now in the developed world, unless there is a remarkable change in the economy of owning a PC. Any technology that requires the masses to own a PC, in its present form, to access information is unlikely to be successful in the foreseeable future. Possibilities appear to exist, however, in the mobile phone technology, which is fast becoming very affordable by the masses, is voice based and can be integrated with the Information Technology at the server end of a computer network. For example, in the field of education people can ask question through a mobile phone, a database of answers to such questions can be generated using the technologies used currently in Wikipedia and call centers and the text in these databases could be converted into voice, by developing text to voice technologies in the various Indian languages. The person seeking information can be informed when the answer is available and better answers sought based on his/her feedback. The emerging 3G and 4G mobile phone technologies can indeed facilitate such developments. An alternative technology could be to integrate the mobile phone with the television screen, so that visual information can be viewed easily. Similarly, there is a possibility for developing interactive radio, on the lines of interactive TV.

MODEL QUESTIONS

1. What are the Advantages/Achievements of ICT in Education Sector?
2. What are the limitations of ICT in the context of a developing country?

REFERENCES

1. http://en.wikipedia.org/wiki/Information_ communication_technology#PC-based_ICT
2. http://en.wikipedia.org/wiki/Information_communication_technology
3. http://en.wikipedia.org/wiki/Information_technology

10

Electronic Learning

Electronic Learning (or e-Learning or eLearning) is a type of Technology supported education/learning (TSL) where the medium of instruction is computer technology. In some instances, no in-person interaction takes place. *E-learning* is used interchangeably in a wide variety of contexts. In companies, it refers to the strategies that use the company network to deliver training courses to employees. In the USA, it is defined as a planned teaching/learning experience that uses a wide spectrum of technologies, mainly Internet or computer-based, to reach learners. Lately in most Universities, e-learning is used to define a specific mode to attend a course or programmes of study where the students rarely, if ever, attend face-to-face for on-campus access to educational facilities, because they study online.

Growth of e-Learning

By 2006, nearly 3.5 million students were participating in on-line learning at institutions of higher education in the United States. Many higher education, for-profit institutions, now offer on-line classes. By contrast, only about half of private, non-profit schools offer them. The Sloan report, based on a poll of academic leaders, says that students generally appear to be at least as satisfied with their on-line classes as they are with traditional ones. Private institutions may become more involved with on-line presentations as the cost of instituting such a system decreases. Properly trained staff must also be hired to work with students on-line. These staff members need to understand the content area, and also be highly trained in the use of the computer and Internet. Online education is rapidly increasing, and online doctoral programmes have even developed at leading research universities.

Technology

As early as 1993, *Graziadei,* W.D. described an online computer-delivered lecture, tutorial and assessment project using electronic Mail, two VAX Notes conferences and Gopher/Lynx together with several software programmes that allowed students and instructor to create a Virtual Instructional Classroom Environment in Science (VICES) in Research, Education, Service and Teaching (REST). In 1997 Graziadei, W.D., *et al.*, published an article entitled "Building Asynchronous and Synchronous Teaching-Learning Environments: Exploring a Course/Classroom Management System Solution." They described a process at the State University of New York (SUNY) of evaluating products and developing an overall strategy for technology-based course development and management in teaching-learning. The product(s) had to be easy to use and maintain, portable, replicable, scalable, and immediately affordable, and they had to have a high probability of success with long-term cost-effectiveness. Today many technologies can be, and are, used in e-Learning, from blogs to collaborative software, ePortfolios, and virtual classrooms. Most eLearning situations use combinations of the these techniques.

Along with the terms *learning technology, instructional technology,* and Educational Technology, the term is generally used to refer to the use of technology in learning in a much broader sense than the computer-based training or *Computer Aided Instruction* of the 1980s. It is also broader than the terms *Online Learning* or *Online Education* which generally refer to purely web-based learning. In cases where mobile technologies are used, the term M-learning has become more common. E-learning, however, also has implications beyond just the technology and refers to the actual learning that takes place using these systems.

E-learning is naturally suited to distance learning and flexible learning, but can also be used in conjunction with face-to-face teaching, in which case the term Blended learning is commonly used. E-Learning pioneer Bernard Luskin argues that the "E" must be understood to have broad meaning if e-Learning is to be effective. Luskin says that the "e" should be interpreted to mean exciting, energetic, enthusiastic, emotional, extended, excellent, and educational in addition to "electronic" that is a traditional national interpretation. This broader interpretation allows for 21st century applications and brings learning and media psychology into the equation.

In higher education especially, the increasing tendency is to create a Virtual Learning Environment (VLE) (which is sometimes combined with a Management Information System (MIS) to create a Managed Learning Environment) in which all aspects of a course are handled through a consistent user interface standard throughout the institution. A growing number of physical universities, as well as newer online-only colleges, have begun to offer a select set of academic degree and certificate programmes via the Internet at a wide range of levels and in a wide range of disciplines. While some programmes require students to attend some campus classes or orientations, many are delivered completely online. In addition, several universities offer online student support services, such as online advising and registration, e-counseling, online textbook purchase, student governments and student newspapers.

E-Learning can also refer to educational websites such as those offering learning scenarios, worksheets and interactive exercises for children. The term is also used extensively in the business sector where it generally refers to cost-effective online training.

Services

E-learning services have evolved since computers were first used in education. There is a trend to move toward blended learning services, where computer-based activities are integrated with practical or classroom-based situations.

Goals of e-Learning

E-Learning lessons are generally designed to guide students through information or to help students perform in specific tasks. Information based e-Learning content communicates information to the student. Examples include content that distributes the history or facts related to a service, company, or product. In information-based content, there is no specific skill to be learned. In performance-based content, the lessons build off of a procedural skill in which the student is expected to increase proficiency.

Computer-Based Learning

Computer Based Learning, sometimes abbreviated to CBL, refers to the use of computers as a key component of the educational environment. While this can refer to the use of computers in a classroom, the term more broadly refers to a structured environment in which computers are used for teaching purposes. The concept is generally seen as being distinct from the use of computers in ways where learning is at least a peripheral element of the experience (e.g. computer games and web browsing).

Computer-Based Training (CBT) services are where a student learns by executing special training programmes on a computer relating to their occupation. CBT is especially effective for training people to use computer applications because the CBT programme can be integrated with the applications so that students can practice using the application as they learn. Historically, CBTs growth has been hampered by the enormous resources required: human resources to create a CBT programme, and hardware resources needed to run it. However, the increase in PC computing power, and especially the growing prevalence of computers equipped with CD-ROMs, is making CBT a more viable option for corporations and individuals alike. Many PC applications now come with some modest form of CBT, often called a tutorial. Web-Based Training (WBT) is a type of training that is similar to CBT; however, it is delivered over the Internet using a web browser. Web-based training frequently includes interactive methods, such as bulletin boards, chat rooms, instant messaging, videoconferencing, and discussion threads. Web-based training is usually a self-paced learning medium though some systems allow for online testing and evaluation at specific times.

Pedagogical Elements

Pedagogical elements are an attempt to define structures or units of educational material. For example, this could be a lesson, an assignment, a multiple choice question, a quiz, a discussion group or a case study. These units should be format independent, so although it may be implemented in any of the following methods, pedagogical structures would *not* include a textbook, a web page, a video conference or Podcast.

When beginning to create e-Learning content, the pedagogical approaches need to be evaluated. Simple pedagogical approaches make it easy to create content, but lack flexibility, richness and downstream functionality. On the other hand, complex pedagogical approaches can be difficult to set up and slow to develop, though they have the potential to provide more engaging learning experiences for students. Somewhere between these extremes is an ideal pedagogy that allows a particular educator to effectively create educational materials while simultaneously providing the most engaging educational experiences for students.

Pedagogical Approaches or Perspectives

It is possible to use various pedagogical approaches for eLearning which include:

- *Instructional Design*— the traditional pedagogy of instruction which is curriculum focused, and is developed by a centralized educating group or a single teacher.
- *Social-Constructivist*—this pedagogy is particularly well afforded by the use of discussion forums, blogs, wiki and on-line collaborative activities. It is a collaborative approach that opens educational content creation to a wider group including the students themselves.
- *Laurillard's Conversational Model*—is also particularly relevant to eLearning, and Gilly Salmon's Five-Stage Model is a pedagogical approach to the use of discussion boards.
- *Cognitive Perspective*—focuses on the cognitive processes involved in learning as well as how the brain works.
- *Emotional Perspective*—focuses on the emotional aspects of learning, like motivation, engagement, fun, etc.
- *Behavioural Perspective*—focuses on the skills and behavioural outcomes of the learning process. Role-playing and application to on-the-job settings.
- *Contextual Perspective*—focuses on the environmental and social aspects which can stimulate learning. Interaction with other people, collaborative discovery and the importance of peer support as well as pressure.

Reusability, Standards and Learning Objects

Much effort has been put into the technical re-use of electronically-based teaching materials and in particular creating or re-using *Learning Objects*. These are self-contained units that are properly tagged with keywords, or other meta data, and often stored in an XML file format. Creating a course requires putting together a sequence of learning objects. There are both proprietary and open, non-commercial and commercial, peer-reviewed repositories of learning objects such as the Merlot repository.

A common standard format for e-learning content is SCORM whilst other specifications allow for the transporting of "learning objects" (Schools Interoperability Framework) or categorizing meta-data (LOM).

These standards themselves are early in the maturity process with the oldest being 8 years old. They are also relatively vertical specific: SIF is primarily pK-12, LOM is primarily Corp, Military and Higher Ed, and SCORM is primarily Military and Corp with some Higher Ed. PESC-the Post-Secondary Education Standards Council-is also making headway in developing standards and learning objects for the Higher Ed space, while SIF is beginning to seriously turn towards Instructional and Curriculum learning objects.

In the US pK-12 space there are a host of content standards that are critical as well-the NCES data standards are a prime example. Each State Government's content standards and achievement benchmarks are critical metadata for linking e-learning objects in that space.

An excellent example of e-learning that relates to knowledge management and reusability is Navy E-Learning, which is available to Active Duty, Retired, or Disable Military members. This on-line tool provides certificate courses to enrich the user in various subjects related to military training and civilian skill sets. The e-learning system not only provides learning objectives, but also evaluates the progress of the student and credit can be earned toward higher learning institutions. This reuse is an excellent example of knowledge retention and the cyclical process of knowledge transfer and use of data and records.

Communication Technologies Used in e-Learning

Communication technologies are generally categorized as asynchronous or synchronous. *Asynchronous* activities use technologies such as blogs, wikis, and discussion boards. The idea here is that participants may engage in the exchange of ideas or information without the dependency of other participants involvement at the same time. Electronic mail (E-mail) is also asynchronous in that mail can be sent or received without having both the participants' involvement at the same time.

Synchronous activities involve the exchange of ideas and information with one or more participants during the same period

remote control, lecture broadcasting, board meetings, virtual labs and anonymous drug, rape and depression counseling. The announcement stated TBS will assist member business schools and their associated colleges and universities with implementation planning and rollout assistance to help increase the success of e-learning initiatives. The announcement also stated WebTrain will provide their hosted services free to the business school and their associated college or university for a fiscal school year to reduce financial risk related to using an enterprise class hosted service.

Computer-aided Assessment and Learning Design

Computer-aided Assessment (also but less commonly referred to as E-assessment), ranging from automated multiple-choice tests to more sophisticated systems is becoming increasingly common. With some systems, feedback can be geared towards a student's specific mistakes or the computer can navigate the student through a series of questions adapting to what the student appears to have learned or not learned.

The best examples follow a Formative Assessment structure and are called "Online Formative Assessment." This involves making an initial formative assessment by sifting out the incorrect answers. The author/teacher will then explain what the pupil should have done with each question. It will then give the pupil at least one practice at each slight variation of sifted out questions. This is the formative learning stage. The next stage is to make a Summative Assessment by a new set of questions only covering the topics previously taught. Some will take this even further and repeat the cycle such as BOFA which is aimed at the Eleven plus exam set in the UK.

The term *learning design* has sometimes come to refer to the type of activity enabled by software such as the open-source system LAMS which supports sequences of activities that can be both adaptive and collaborative. The IMS Learning Design specification is intended as a standard format for learning designs, and IMS LD Level A is supported in LAMS V2.

Benefits of eLearning Versus Traditional Classroom Settings

eLearning can provide for major benefits for the organizations and individuals involved.

1. ***Reducing environmental impact:*** eLearning allows people to avoid travel, thus reducing the overall carbon output. The

fact that it takes place in a virtual environment also allows some reduction of paper usage. With virtual notes instead of paper notes and online assessments instead of paper assessments, eLearning is a more environmentally friendly solution.

2. ***Quality education, made affordable:*** The fact that instructors of the highest calibre can share their knowledge across borders allows students to attend courses across physical, political, and economic boundaries. Recognized experts have the opportunity of making information available internationally, to anyone interested at minimum costs. This can drastically reduce the costs of higher education, making it much more affordable and accessible to the masses. An internet connection, a computer, and a projector would allow an entire classroom in a third world university to benefit from the knowledge of an opinion leader.

MODEL QUESTIONS

1. What do you mean by e-learning? How it different from traditional learning?
2. What are the benefits of e-learning?
3. What are the pedagogical aspects of e-learning?

REFERENCES

1. Daniel, J.S. (1996). *Mega-Universities and Knowledge Media: Technology Strategies for Higher Education*, Kogan Page, London.
2. Gold, L. & Maitland, C. (1999). What's the difference? A review of contemporary research on the effectiveness of distance learning in higher education. Washington, DC: NEA.
3. Hebert, D.G. (2007). "Five Challenges and Solutions in Online Music Teacher Education," Research and Issues in Music Education, Vol. 5,
4. http://en.wikipedia.org/wiki/E-learning
5. Merriam, S., Caffarella, R., & Baumgartner, L. (2007). Learning in Adulthood New York: Wiley.
6. Moore, Michael G.; Greg Kearsley (2005). *Distance Education: A Systems View*, Second, Belmont, CA: Wadsworth.
7. White, M. (1982). 'Distance Education in Australian Higher Education — a History', *Distance Education*, Vol. 3.

11

Virtual Education

Virtual education refers to instruction in a learning environment where teacher and student are separated by time or space, or both, and the teacher provides course content through course management applications, multimedia resources, the Internet, videoconferencing, etc. Students receive the content and communicate with the teacher via the same technologies.

Characteristics of Virtual Education

Virtual education is a term describing online education using the Internet. This term is primarily used in higher education where so-called Virtual Universities have been established.

Virtual courses—a synonym is online courses—are courses delivered on the Internet. "Virtual" is used here to characterize the fact that the course is not taught in a classroom face-to-face but through some substitute mode that can be associated with classroom teaching.

A virtual programme (or a virtual course of studies) is a study programme in which all courses or at least a significant portion of the courses are virtual courses.

Instruction Modes for Virtual Education

Many virtual study programmes are mainly text based, using HTML, PowerPoint, or PDF documents. Multimedia technologies have been investigated for many years and eventually found their way into practice. Today a wide spectrum of instruction modes is available, including the following:

- *Virtual classroom:* A virtual classroom is a learning environment created in the virtual space. The objectives of a virtual classroom are to improve access to advanced educational experiences by allowing students and instructors to participate in remote learning communities using personal computers; and to improve the quality and effectiveness of education by using the computer to support a collaborative learning process. The explosion of the knowledge age has changed the context of what is learnt and how it is learnt—the concept of virtual classrooms is a manifestation of this knowledge revolution.
- *Hypertext courses:* Structured course material is used as in a conventional distance education programme. However, all material is provided electronically and can be viewed with a browser. Hyperlinks connect text, multimedia parts and exercises in a meaningful way.
- *Video-based courses:* Are like face-to-face classroom courses, with a lecturer speaking and PowerPoint slides or online examples used for illustration. Video-streaming technologies is used. Students watch the video by means of freeware or plug-ins (e.g. Windows Media Player, RealPlayer).
- *Audio-based courses:* Are similar but instead of moving pictures only the sound track of the lecturer is provided. Often the course pages are enhanced with a text transcription of the lecture.
- *Animated courses:* Enriching text-oriented or audio-based course material by animations is generally a good way of making the content and its appearance more interesting. Animations are created using Macromedia Flash or similar technologies.
- *Web-supported textbook courses:* Are based on specific textbooks. Students read and reflect the chapters by themselves. Review questions, topics for discussion, exercises, case studies, etc. are given chapterwise on a website and discussed with the lecturer. Class meetings may be held to discuss matters in a chatroom.
- *Peer-to-peer courses*: Are courses taught "on-demand" and without a prepared curriculum. A new field of online education has emerged in 2007 through new online education platforms.

Communication and Interaction

Students in virtual education typically acquire knowledge in a uni-directional manner first (e.g. by studying a video, reading a textbook chapter). Subsequent discussions of problems, solving exercises, case studies, review questions, etc. help the students to understand better what they learned before. Electronic media like a discussion forum, chat room, voice mail, e-mail, etc. are often employed for communication.

Homework assignments are normally submitted electronically, e.g. as an attachment to an e-mail. When help is needed, lecturers, tutors, or fellow students, or a help desk are available, just like in a real university. The difference is that all communication goes via electronic media.

Platforms

Most virtual study programmes use an e-learning platform (Learning Management System—LMS) to administer students and courses and to provide learning content. Most notable are WebCT and Moodle.

- Second Life has recently become a virtual classroom for major colleges and universities, including Princeton, Rice University, University of Derby (UK), Vassar, the Open University (UK). In 2007 Second Life started to be used for foreign language tuition Both Second Life and real life language educators have begun to use the virtual world for language tuition. English (as a foreign language) has gained a presence through several schools, including the British Council, which has focused on the Teen Grid. Spain's language and cultural institute, the Instituto Cervantes has an island on Second Life.
- WebEx is also increasingly used as an online learning platform and classroom for a diverse set of education providers such as Fox School of Business for Templer University, Grades Grow, Minnesota State Colleges and Universities, and Sachem. Webex is a Cisco Web Meetings and Collaboration Solution. The platform has worked for educational institutions because of real time collaboration using an interactive whiteboard, chat, and VOIP technology that allows audio and video sharing. In distance learning situations, while replacing the classroom with features, institutions have also looked for security features which are

inherently strong in a Cisco powered collaboration environment. The downside is that Webex is not a free platform.

Virtual School/Cyber School

A *virtual school* or *cyberschool* describes an institution that teaches courses entirely or primarily through online methods. Though there are tens of thousands of commercial and non-accredited courses available online, the term "virtual school" is generally reserved for accredited schools that teach a full-time (or nearly full-time) course of instruction designed to lead to a degree. At the primary and secondary level, accreditation means that virtual schools tend to receive public funding; some publicly funded and private universities also provide accredited online degrees.

All student services are conducted through Internet technology. The virtual school differ/contrasts from the traditional school through the physical media that links administrators, teachers and students and is an alliance of public distance learning schools. Many states in the United States have their own virtual school, and many of them have students numbering in the thousands. By providing a student's social security number the person is then entered into a database where they can chose which classes they want to take.

There are many different virtual school instructional and enrollment models. Instructional models range from fully independent self paced courses to semester based, teacher facilitated courses. Class sizes range widely with anywhere from 25 students to as many as 200 students in each class section. Students keep in contact with teachers and collaborate with other students through web communication tools provided in the course delivery platforms like Blackboard or Moodle. In some cases students communicate by phone with instructors. To help with communication many virtual schools have implemented their own system programmes to help build courses and maintain student profiles. There are also many books and training manuals to aid in the development of such schools and courses.

History

Many of today's virtual schools are descendants of corres-pondence schools. Sometimes referred to as "distance learning," correspondence schools offered students an alternative to the traditional brick and mortar meetings within a schoolhouse. These schools utilized the postal service for student-teacher interaction, or used two-way radio transmissions, sometimes with pre-recorded television broadcasts. Students were expected to study their learning material independently and, in some cases, meet with a proctor to be tested. Modern virtual schools provide similar alternatives to students with a more ubiquitous and, often, interactive approach.

Virtual Schools now exist all around the world. Some of these virtual schools have been integrated into public schools (particularly in the United States), where students sit in computer labs and do their work online. In other situations, students can be completely homeschooled, or they can take any combination of public/private/homeschooling and online classes.

Pricing and Location

Virtual schools may be free if the state pays for the courses, otherwise, there will be a course fee to be paid for by the student, parents or student's home school. Other materials would be purchased by the student, such as books.

Materials can also add up. Most courses will provide electronic materials free of cost, but others require some shopping on the students part. Textbooks are not required but can be used as an aid for coursework.

Materials

As mentioned earlier, many materials are provided free of cost. Some schools provide high quality programmes, usually for web design classes. Some popular materials include Adobe products, Jasc products, and products from Macromedia. Other schools may use Corel products as a cheaper alternative. These products are usually free. You usually receive the full version of the selected programme, with a limited license, usually 1 year or so. These programmes are key in the success of virtual schools, and help them to improve each year. Many schools will also provide a brand new computer for all students in need of one. Generally, these computers run using the Microsoft operating system, Windows XP, but depending on your needs and coursework the school may also use Linux based computers or Apple Macintoshes.

Advantages and Disadvantages

One advantage of cyberschools is that a person does not have to travel to a real classroom to learn.

Another advantage is that online learning creates the opportunity for integrating digital media into the curriculum in an interactive format making teaching and learning more student centered.

Disadvantages include that a person must be self motivated to learn as learning cannot be enforced via the internet in the asynchronous model; and for the synchronous model, "lack of socialization" is often quoted, but recent anecdotal evidence from one live cyberschool indicates that, while socialization may be different, it is not lacking.

Grading

Generally, grading is controlled by the teachers. There are four main types of assignments. Assessments are the most common, and include students uploading files, usually created using word processors or spreadsheets. Worksheets are also common, and can consist of multiple choice, matching, short answer, and other questions. Most questions from worksheets are auto graded by the computer, but if a response is needed for any question, the teacher must manually grade that portion of the assignment. Discussions are common too. They usually have a very small grade value, and usually don't show up in the assignments section of the course, where you submit work and check scores. The final type of assignment is exams. These assignments usually count for a large part of the student's grade, and are usually taken at the end of modules, or at the mid-term point or final portion of a class.

The scoring system is generally the same as any public school system in the United States. In most schools a letter grade of *A* is accomplished when a student's number grade is between 90 and 100 per cent. A score of 80 to 89 per cent will earn a *B*, and so on. An *F* is the lowest score you can earn, and encompasses scores of 50 per cent or below in most cases.

MODEL QUESTIONS

1. What are the Instruction modes adopted in virtual education?
2. What are the advantages and limitations of cyber learning?
3. What are the characteristics of virtual education?

REFERENCES

1. BBC News Article "Families enrol for online school."
2. Briteschool FAQ "Disadvantages of attending an online school."
3. Dorveaux, Xavier (2007-07-15). "Apprendre une langue dans un monde virtuel", Le Monde. Retrieved on 15 July 2007.
4. http://en.wikipedia.org/wiki/Virtual_education
5. http://en.wikipedia.org/wiki/Virtual_school
6. Kurbel, Karl: Virtuality on the Students' and on the Teachers' sides: A Multimedia and Internet based International Master Programme; ICEF Berlin GmbH (Eds.), Proceedings on the 7th International Conference on Technology Supported Learning and Training - Online Educa; Berlin, Germany; November 2001, pp. 133–136.
7. Loutchko, Iouri; Kurbel, Karl; Pakhomov, Alexei: Production and Delivery of Multimedia Courses for Internet Based Virtual Education; The World Congress "Networked Learning in a Global Environment: Challenges and Solutions for Virtual Education", Berlin, Germany, May 1-4, 2002.
8. Parker, Quin (2007-04-06). "A second look at school life", The Guardian. Retrieved on 16 June 2007.

12

Challenges in Integrating ICTs in Education

On the basis of lessons learned from best practices around the world, there is no other formula for determining the optimal level of ICT integration in the educational system. Significant challenges that policy-makers and planners, educators, education administrators, and other stakeholders need to consider include educational policy and planning, infrastructure, language and content, capacity building, and financing.

Implications of ICT-Enhanced Education for Educational Policy and Planning

Attempts to enhance and reform education through ICTs require clear and specific objectives, guidelines and time-bound targets, the mobilization of required resources, and the political commitment at all levels to see the initiative stage. Some essential elements of planning for ICT are listed below:

(a) A rigorous analysis of the present state of the educational system. ICT-based interventions must take into account current institutional practices and arrangements. Specifically, drivers and barriers to ICT use need to be identified, including those related to curriculum and pedagogy, infrastructure, capacity-building, language and content, and financing.

(b) The specification of educational goals at different education and training levels as well as the different modalities of use of ICTs that can best be employed in pursuit of these goals. This requires of the policymaker an understanding of the potentials of different ICTs when applied in different contexts

for different purposes, and an awareness of priority education needs and financial and human resource capacity and constraints within the country or locality, as well as best practices around the world and how these practices can be adapted for specific country requirements.

(c) The identification of stakeholders and the harmonizing of efforts across different interest groups.

(d) The piloting of the chosen ICT-based model. Even the best designed models or those that have already been proven to work in other contexts need to be tested on a small scale. Such pilots are essential to identify, and correct, potential glitches in instructional design, implementability, effectiveness, and the like.

(e) The specification of existing sources of financing and the development of strategies for generating financial resources to support ICT use over the long term.

Infrastructure-Related Challenges in ICT-Enhanced Education

A country's educational technology infrastructure sits on top of the national telecommunications and information infrastructure. Before any ICT-based programme is launched, policy-makers and planners must carefully consider the following:

- In the first place, are appropriate rooms or buildings available to house the technology? In countries where there are many old school buildings, extensive retrofitting to ensure proper electrical wiring, heating/cooling and ventilation, and safety and security would be needed.
- Another basic requirement is the availability of electricity and telephony. In developing countries large areas are still without a reliable supply of electricity and the nearest telephones are miles away. Experience in some countries in Africa point to wireless technologies (such as VSAT or Very Small Aperture Terminal) as possible levers for leapfrogging. Although this is currently an extremely costly approach, other developing countries with very poor telecommunications infrastructure should study this option.
- Policy-makers should also look at the ubiquity of different types of ICT in the country in general, and in the educational system (at all levels) in particular. For instance, a basic requirement for computer-based or online learning is access

to computers in schools, communities, and households, as well as affordable Internet service.

In general, ICT use in education should follow use in society, not lead it. Education programmes that use cutting-edge technologies rarely achieve long term success: It is cheaper, and easier, to introduce a form of technology into education, and keep it working, where education is riding on the back of large-scale developments by governments or the private sector. Television works for education when it follows rather than precedes television for entertainment; computers in schools can be maintained once commercial and private use has expanded to the point where there is an established service industry.

Challenges with Respect to Capacity-Building

Various competencies must be developed throughout the educational system for ICT integration to be successful.

Teachers: Teacher professional development should have five foci:

1. skills with particular applications
2. integration into existing curricula
3. curricular changes related to the use of IT (including changes in instructional design)
4. changes in teacher role; and
5. underpinning educational theories. Ideally, these should be addressed in pre-service teacher training and built on and enhanced in-service. In some countries, like Singapore, Malaysia, and the United Kingdom, teaching accreditation requirements include training in ICT use.

Will ICTs Replace the Teacher?

The answer is a resounding NO! In fact, with the introduction of ICTs in the classroom, the teacher's role in the learning process becomes even more critical. What can and should change is the kind of role that the teacher plays. The role of students, in turn, also expands. And since ICTs can open up the classroom to the outside world, the community can also play a new role in the classroom. As learning shifts from the "teacher-centered model" to a "learner-centered model", the teacher becomes less the sole voice of authority and more the facilitator, mentor and coach-from "sage on stage" to "guide on the side."

The teacher's primary task becomes to teach the students how to ask questions and pose problems, formulate hypotheses, locate information and then critically assess the information found in relation to the problems posed. And since ICT-enhanced learning is a new experience even for the teachers, the teachers become co-learners and discover new things along with their students.

Additionally, it is not uncommon to see students in an ICT-enabled classroom assume both formal and informal roles as teachers of their peers and younger students, sometimes even of their own teachers. Teachers and students from different schools, subject-matter experts, parents, community and business leaders, politicians, and other interested parties also become involved in the learning process-as resource persons, critics, mentors, and cheerleaders. They also comprise a public, and hopefully critical, audience for students' work published on the Web or through other media.

Yet many teachers are reluctant to use ICTs, especially computers and the Internet. Hannafin and Savenye identify some of the reasons for this reluctance: poor software design, skepticism about the effectiveness of computers in improving learning outcomes, lack of administrative support, increased time and effort needed to learn the technology and how to use it for teaching, and the fear of losing their authority in the classroom as it becomes more learner-centered. These are all issues that must be addressed by both pre-service teacher education and in-service teacher professional development programmes if schools and other educational institutions are to fully exploit the potential of computers and the Internet as educational tools at the in-service level, ICT Teacher Professional Development (TPD) should be long-term, teacher-directed, and as flexible as possible. For many under-qualified, overworked, and underpaid teachers in developing countries, effective adoption of ICTs hinges on being given continuous opportunities to learn what they need to learn based on their specific circumstances and experience, when they have the time to learn it. Institutionalized incentives and support for teachers to pursue ICT TPD are also critical. This may take the form of promotions for teachers who innovate with (as opposed to merely using) ICTs in the classroom, or simply making sure that teachers have adequate access to technology after training.

Education Administrators: Leadership plays a key role in ICT integration in education. Many teacher-or student-initiated ICT projects have been undermined by lack of support from above. For ICT integration programmes to be effective and sustainable, administrators themselves must be competent in the use of the technology, and they must have a broad understanding of the technical, curricular, administrative, financial, and social dimensions of ICT use in education.

Technical Support Specialists: Whether provided by in-school staff or external service providers, or both, technical support specialists are essential to the continued viability of ICT use in a given school.

World Links for Development (WorLD)

The World Links for Development (WorLD) Programme began in Uganda in 1997 under the auspices of the World Bank Institute. Its goal was to help government to bring the benefits of the Internet and the World Wide Web to the country's secondary schools. The WorLD Programme has three components: Connectivity, Training, and Monitoring and Evaluation. While many international and local organizations have focused on providing technology to schools, World has, over the years, built an impressive reputation as one of the world's leading providers of professional development services to teachers, school administrators and policy-makers in developing countries around the world. World's Professional Development Programme for Teachers, which is delivered primarily face-to-face by international and local trainers, with follow-ups online, are in five phases:

Phase 0. Computer Literacy

Objective: To introduce the fundamentals of computer technology and help participants acquire basic computer literacy knowledge and skills.

Phase 1. Introduction to the Internet for Teaching and Learning

Objective: Introduce fundamental concepts, technologies, and skills necessary for introducing networked technology and the Internet to teaching and learning; initiate discussion of new possibilities, generate basic e-mail projects.

Phase 2. Introduction to Telecollaborative Learning Projects

Objective: Introduction to educational telecollaboration–from activity structures to the creation, design, implementation and dissemination of original projects.

Phase 3. Curriculum and Technology Integration

Objective: Develop skills and understanding of how to create, incorporate and facilitate innovative classroom practices that integrate networked technology and curricula.

Phase 4. Innovations: Pedagogy, Technology and Professional Development

Objective: Develop skills and understanding of how to evaluate and diffuse innovative classroom practices while addressing social and ethical concerns. World has also developed training models for policy-makers on educational ICT management and on telecenters. World is currently active in over 20 countries in Africa, Latin America and South Asia. It is set to roll out its programme in Southeast Asia-in Cambodia, Laos, Vietnam, Indonesia and the Philippines—in 2003.

Without on-site technical support, much time and money may be lost due to technical breakdowns.

In the Philippines, for example, one of the major obstacles to optimizing computer use in high schools has been the lack of timely technical support. In some extreme cases involving schools in remote areas, disabled computers take months to be repaired since no technician is available in the immediate vicinity and so the computers have to be sent to the nearest city hundreds of kilometers away.

Content Developers

Content development is a critical area that is too often overlooked. The bulk of existing ICT-based educational material is likely to be in English or of little relevance to education in developing countries (especially at the primary and secondary levels). There is a need to develop original educational content (e.g., radio programmes, interactive multimedia learning materials on CD-ROM or DVD, Web-based courses, etc.), adapt existing content, and convert print-based content to digital media. These are tasks for which content development specialists such as instructional designers, scriptwriters, audio and video production specialists, programmers, multimedia course authors, and web-developers are needed. Like technical support specialists, content developers are highly skilled professionals and are not, with the exception of instructional designers, historically employed by primary and secondary schools. Many universities with distance education programmes, and those who otherwise make use of ICTs, have dedicated technical support and content development units.

Challenges Need to be Addressed in the Areas of Language and Content

English is the dominant language of the Internet. An estimated 80 per cent of online content is in English. A large proportion of the educational software produced in the world market is in English. For developing countries in the Asia-Pacific where English language proficiency is not high, especially outside metropolitan areas, this represents a serious barrier to maximizing the educational benefits of the World Wide Web. Even in countries where English is a second language (such as Singapore, Malaysia, the Philippines, and India) it is imperative that teaching and learning materials that match national curriculum requirements and have locally meaningful content, preferably in the local languages, be developed. This would ensure that the Web is a genuinely multicultural space and that peoples of different cultures have an equal stake and voice in the global communities of learning and practice online.

Particularly vulnerable to exclusion of this sort are isolated, rural populations, cultural minorities, and women in general. Thus attention must be paid to their special needs. One encouraging trend has been the emergence of national and regional school networks, or School Nets, that facilitate the sharing of content and information-curriculum guides, teaching and learning resources, telecollaborative project registries, school and teacher directories, training curricula and materials, research and policy papers, technology management guides, and start-up toolkits, among others. Countries like Australia, France, Finland, Japan, Canada, Thailand, Ghana, South Africa and Zimbabwe, to name a few, all have national SchoolNets. The Enlaces programme in Latin America has linked schools from Spanish-speaking countries like Chile, Paraguay, Costa Rica, Colombia, and Peru. In Southeast Asia, efforts are currently underway to pilot SchoolNets in the Philippines, Indonesia, Cambodia, Laos, Myanmar and Vietnam, and to link these to existing national SchoolNets to create a region-wide ASEAN SchoolNet.

In Web-based learning, technical standardization of content has also become a pressing issue. Standardization allows different applications to share content and learning systems. Specifications in content, structure, and test formats are proposed so that interoperability may exist between different management systems, resulting in some cost-efficiencies. Standards must be general enough to support all kinds of learning systems and content. Worth mentioning are initiatives conducted by the Instructional Management System (IMS), the Advanced Distributed Learning / Shareable Courseware Object Reference Model (ADL/SCORM) initiative, the Aviation Industry Computer Based Training Committee (AICC), and the European ARIADNE project, since some of the standards they have proposed are already being widely applied.

The ease by which Web-based educational content can be stored, transmitted, duplicated, and modified has also raised concerns about the protection of intellectual property rights. For instance, intellectual, property rights violated when lectures broadcast over the television or on the Web incorporate pre-existing materials, or when students record educational broadcast on tape for later viewing? While schools and universities may already have agreements that expressly authorize the use of certain materials for classroom purposes, these agreements may not be broad enough to accommodate telecommunications transmission, videotape recording, or the distribution of course-related materials beyond the classroom setting.

The United Nations International World Intellectual Property Organization is leading international efforts in setting global standards for the protection of intellectual property rights that would not at the same time unduly curtail the accessing and sharing of information. For teachers and students, each of whom are potential publishers of multimedia materials that incorporate the works of others, information and training about the ethical use of intellectual property should be an important component of ICT-based programmes.

Challenges Related to Financing the Cost of ICT Use

One of the greatest challenges in ICT use in education is balancing educational goals with economic realities. ICTs in education programmes require large capital investments and developing countries need to be prudent in making decisions about what models of ICT use will be introduced and to be conscious of maintaining economies of scale. Ultimately it is an issue of whether the value added of ICT use offsets the cost, relative to the cost of alternatives. Put another way, is ICT-based learning the most effective strategy for achieving the desired educational goals, and if so what is the modality and scale of implementation that can be supported given existing financial, human and other resources?

Content is King: Lessons from Thailand

Three years after its inception in 1995, SchoolNet Thailand, a joint project of the National Electronics and Computer Technology Center (NECTEC), the Telephone Organization of Thailand, the Communications Authority of Thailand, and the Ministry of Education, found itself facing a challenge it had not entirely expected. Having built a network infrastructure for education in Thailand that connected 152 local secondary schools to the Internet, it discovered that schools hardly used the Internet as a tool for teaching and learning. It soon became apparent that the lack of quality educational online resources in the local language, Thai, was discouraging Internet use among teachers and students. SchoolNet Thailand thus had to expand what had largely been a "universal access" programme to include content development-complemented by training-in the Thai language. In September 1998, SchoolNet Thailand commissioned Kasetstart University and the Institute for the Promotion of Teaching Science and Technology to create Thai language websites on secondary school-level Mathematics, Physics, Chemistry, Biology, Engineering, the Environment, and Computer Science. Collectively called the "Digital Library", these websites were launched a little over a year later. SchoolNet Thailand also developed an easy-to-use web authoring application called the "Digital Library Tool Kit" that allowed teachers to create Web-based lessons in Thai. Teachers and students were also given instruction on web page development. By May 2001, the Digital Library already contained 1,113 lessons, created mostly by classroom teachers. Complementing the "Digital Library" project was the production of multimedia professional development materials called "Thai Teacher 2000" which included a printed manual, a video tape, and a CD-ROM.

SchoolNet Thailand's content development efforts also benefited from a national documentation project spearheaded by the Office of the National Cultural Commission called "Thai Cultural Information System." This programme was intended to, among others, collect information on Thai culture and disseminate this information through CD-ROMs and the Internet.

At present, SchoolNet Thailand boasts of approximately 4,000 schools in its network, with over 900 of these with their own web pages in Thai. It expects to extend Internet service provision to the estimated 34,000 schools nationwide in the coming years and to continue to lead in local content development in Thailand.

Whyte suggests the following potential sources of money and resources for ICT use programmes:

1. Grants
2. Public subsidies
3. Private donations, fund-raising events
4. In-kind support (e.g., equipment, volunteers)
5. Community support (e.g., rent-free building)
6. Membership fees
7. Revenues earned from core business:
   - Connectivity (phone, fax, Internet, web pages)
   - Direct computer access to users
   - Office services (photocopying, scanning, audiovisual aids)
8. Revenues earned from ancillary activities:
   - Business services (word-processing, spreadsheets, budget preparation, printing, reception services)
   - Educational services (distant education, training courses)
   - Community services (meeting rooms, social events, local information, remittances from migrant workers)
   - Telework and consulting
   - Specialized activities (telemedicine)
   - Sales (stationary, stamps, refreshments, etc.).

Private sector-public sector partnerships to either pilot or fast track ICT-based projects is a strategy that has gained currency among Ministries of Education in developing countries. These partnerships take many forms, including private sector grants with government counterpart contributions, donations of equipment and education-related content by corporations to state-run schools, and the provision of technical assistance for planning, management, and strengthening human resources at the grassroots level. Multilateral organizations and international aid agencies have also driven many of the most significant ICT in education efforts in the developing world.

But the financial litmus test of ICT-based programmes is survival after donor money has run out. Many ICT based education programmes funded by aid agencies or by corporations could not be sustained because government failed to step in with the necessary financing; nor were the local communities in a position to generate the resources needed to continue these programmes. This was the case with some of the Interactive Radio Instruction projects initiated by USAID. Therefore, a two-fold strategy is key: Government support and local community mobilization.

Will ICT use be the Silver Bullet that will Rid a Developing Country of all of its Educational Problems?

If there is one truism that has emerged in the relatively brief history of ICT use in education, it is this:

> It is not the technology but how you use it! Put another way: "How you use technology is more important than if you use it at all... [and] unless our thinking about schooling changes along with the continuing expansion of [ICTs] in the classroom then our technology investment will fail to live up to its potential."

Technology then should not drive education; rather, educational goals and needs, and careful economics, must drive technology use. Only in this way can educational institutions in developing countries effectively and equitably address the key needs of the population, to help the population as a whole respond to new challenges and opportunities created by an increasingly global economy. ICTs, therefore, cannot by themselves resolve educational problems in the developing world, as such problems are rooted in well entrenched issues of poverty, social inequality, and uneven development. What ICTs as educational tools can do, if they are used prudently, is enable developing countries to expand access to and raise the quality of education. Prudence requires careful consideration of the interacting issues that underpin ICT use in the school-policy and politics, infrastructure development, human capacity, language and content, culture, equity, cost, and not least, curriculum and pedagogy.

MODEL QUESTIONS

1. What are the implications of ICT enhanced education for educational policy and planning?
2. What are the infrastructure related challenges in ICT-enhanced education?
3. What are the challenges with respect to capacity-building?
4. Write a short note on 'WorLD'.

REFERENCES

1. Blurton, C.,"New Directions of ICT-Use in Education". Available online http://www.unesco.org/education/educprog/lwf/dl/edict.pdf.
2. EnGauge. North Central Regional Educational Laboratory; available from http://www.ncrel.org/engauge/skills/21skills.htm.
3. http://www.ignou.ac.in
4. http://www.ignou.ac.in. See also Asian Development Bank (1997), *Distance Education for Primary School Teachers: Papers and Proceedings of the Regional Seminar on Distance Education* (Manila:Asian Development Bank).
5. http://www.open.ac.uk
6. International Center for Distance Learning, "Universitas Terbuka/ Indonesian Open Learning University"; available from http://www-icdl.open.ac.uk/instResult.ihtml?inst_id Victoria L. Tinio, ICT in *Education.*
7. International Labour Organization, "Learning and Training for Work in the Knowledge Society;" available from http://www.Ilo.org/ public/ English/employment/skills/recomm/report.
8. NEC TEC. (July 2002) *ICT for Poverty Reduction*: Examples of Programmes/Projects in Thailand.
9. The Commonwealth of Learning,"An Introduction to Open and Distance Learning"; available from http://www.col.org/ODLIntro/ introODL.htm.
10. US Department of Labour (1999), *Futurework-Trends and Challenges for Work in the 21st Century.*
11. World Bank (1998), *The World Development Report 1998/99. Quoted in Blurton, C., New Directions of ICT-Use in Education.*

13
Convergence of ICT and Education

Information and Communication Technology (ICT) has become, within a very short time, one of the basic building blocks of modern society. Many countries have now begun understanding the importance of ICT and mastering the basic skills and concepts of it as part of the core of education. Organizations, experts and practitioners in the education sector have recognized the importance of ICT in supporting educational improvement and reform. When two technologies are converging, together they will generate some great opportunities and challenges.

The use of information and communication technology in education makes teaching-learning process effective and interesting. To know the impact of ICT in education, we need to know two basic things: ICT, and education.

The *Information and Communication Technology* (ICT) is an umbrella term that includes any communication device or application, encompassing: Radio, television, cellular phones, computer, and network hardware and software, satellite systems and so on, as well as the various services and applications associated with them, such as videoconferencing and distance learning. When such technologies are used for educational purposes, namely to support and improve the learning of students and to develop learning environments, ICT can be considered as a subfield of Educational Technology. Education encompasses teaching and learning specific skills, and also something less tangible but more profound: The imparting of knowledge, positive judgment and well developed wisdom. Education has as one of its fundamental aspects the imparting of culture from generation to generation. Education means 'to draw out' facilitating realization of self potential and latent talents of an individual. It is an application of pedagogy, a body of theoretical and applied research relating to teaching and learning and draws on many disciplines such as psychology, philosophy, computer science, linguistics, neuroscience, sociology and anthropology. In view of ICT, education can be classified in three main categories- E-Learning, Blended Learning, and Distance Learning.

E-Learning

Electronic learning or e-learning is a general term used to refer to computer-enhanced learning. It is commonly associated with the field of Advanced Learning Technology (ALT), which deals with both the technologies and associated methodologies in learning using networked and/or multimedia technologies. It is also known as *online learning*. Distance education provided the base for e-learning's development. E-learning can be "on demand." It overcomes timing, attendance and travel difficulties.

Blended Learning

Blended Learning is the combination of multiple approaches to learning. It is usually used to define a situation where different delivery methods are combined together to deliver a particular course. These methods may include a mixture of face-to-face classrooms, self-paced learning and online classrooms.

(a) Face to Face Learning

Face to face learning refers to learning that occurs in a traditional classroom setting where a faculty member delivers instruction to a group of learners. This could include lectures, workshops, presentations, tutoring, conference and much more.

(b) Self Paced Learning

Self paced learning provides the flexibility to learn according to the availability of learners' own time and pace, it occurs in a variety of ways such as: Reading specific chapters from text book, studying course material presented through web-based or CD-based course, attending prerecorded classes or sessions, reading articles referred by faculty member, working on assignments and projects, and searching and browsing the internet.

(c) Online Collaborative Learning

Online collaboration involves interaction between learners and faculty members through the web; this interaction can occur in one of the following modes:

- Synchronous interaction
- Asynchronous interaction

Synchronous, means "at the same time", it involves interacting with a faculty member and other learners via the Web in real time using technologies such as virtual classrooms and/or chat rooms. On the other hand, Asynchronous means "not at the same time"; it enables learners to interact with their colleagues and faculty member at their own convenience; such as interacting through e-mail.

Distance Learning

It is a type of education, where students work on their own at home or at the office and communicate with faculty and other students via e-mail, electronic forums, videoconferencing, chat rooms, instant messaging and other forms of computer-based communication. It is also known as open learning. Most distance learning programmes include a Computer Based Training (CBT) system and communications tools to produce a virtual *classroom*. Because the Internet and World Wide Web are accessible from virtually all computer platforms, they serve as the foundation for many distance learning systems.

ICT AND LEARNING

ICT needs for successful nationwide institutes computerization programme can be described as a hierarchy.

- Access to modern and stable *ICT infrastructure* by all teachers and students.
- Multifunctional, licensed *software* tools and services for educational use (including Virtual Learning Environments and Content Management Systems).
- ICT *skills* of students and institute staff.
- Integration of ICT into *curriculum* that provides valid goals, content and methods for using ICT in institute.
- *Management* of the ICT innovation on the institute, district, state and national level.

Relationship between Different Kinds of ICT Use in Learning

The relationship between different kinds of ICT use in learning shows that ICT skills for IT jobs, derived from a partial subset of those needed for enhanced living and employment opportunities; and ICT skills for enhanced living and employment opportunities is derived from subset of those ICT skills which are needed for learning in all curriculum areas.

Stages of Teaching and Learning

Teaching and learning process is always going together; we cannot consider these two as separate and independent activities. In fact, these are similar as two sides of the same coin, interconnected and interrelated. The process of teaching and learning in institutes around the world can be divided into four main stages.

Stage 1 – Discovering ICT tools

This stage focuses on discovery of new ICT tools by teachers and students. This is linked with the emerging approach in ICT development.

Stage 2 – Learning how to use ICT tools

This stage emphasizes on learning the use of new ICT tools. It involves the use of general or particular applications of ICT.

Stage 3 – Understanding how and when to use ICT tools

It focuses on understanding how and when to use ICT tools to achieve a particular purpose, such as in completing a given project. This stage indicates the ability to recognize situations where ICT will be helpful, choosing the most appropriate tools for a particular task, and using these tools in combination to solve real problems.

Stage 4 – Specializing in the use of ICT tools

The fourth and last stage involves specializing in the use of ICT tools. This requires deep knowledge about using ICT tools. In this stage students study ICT as a subject to become specialists. Such study concerns vocational or professional education rather than general education.

Opportunities of Integrating ICTs in Education

Modern universities and institutes have a mission to make teaching learning process effective and interesting. Study of use of ICTs in education, reveals the following opportunities:

A. Improved Teaching Learning Process

The traditional way of teaching learning process can be made more effective and interesting by using information and communication technologies. For example, when a teacher uses audio, video, or power point presentations in his/her lecture, the whole class becomes more attentive about the lecture. Such activities also help students to understand the things easily.

B. Increased Availability of Study Material

In traditional learning system, students and teachers are limited to get knowledge on a particular topic through printed materials only. But use of ICT facilitates them to get variety of study materials on a particular topic using internet from any where and at any time.

C. Support for Distance Education and E-Learning

The use of ICT supports distance education and e-learning. Each of the different ICTs-prints, audio/video cassettes, radio and TV broadcasts, computers or the Internet may be used for this purpose. There is a minor difference between distance education and e-learning. The use of ICTs is higher in e-learning than distance learning.

D. Improved Admission and Examination Process

Using ICTs universities and institutes can improve the admission process by putting admission form online and receiving completed form online. They can also generate admit cards for entrance examination online. Even they can conduct entrance and semester/ annual examination online. This will speed up admission and examination process. It also helps in faster result declaration.

E. Help in Research Activities

Application of ICT in education enriches the research activities. Researchers can get information about recent developments in different segments, collect variety of information on a particular topic, and can generate innovative ideas and new findings. Using appropriate software we can easily calculate complex calculations and generate variety of graphs.

Challenges in Integrating ICTs in Education

While considering the opportunities associated with ICT enhanced education it can be said that ICT-enhanced education is better than a simple education, but there are many challenges, which hamper the exploration and exploitation of its opportunities. In view of integrating ICTs in education have following key challenges:

A. ICT Infrastructure

The main challenge for ICT-enhanced education is the availability of information and communication technologies infrastructure. Before any ICT-based programme is launched, policymakers and planners must ensure the availability of the following: appropriate rooms or buildings to house the technology, computers as well as affordable Internet service for on-line learning, and availability of electricity and telephony. In developing countries large areas are still there without reliable supply of electricity and the nearest telephones are miles away.

B. Language and Content

English is the dominant language of the Internet. An estimated 80 per cent of online content is in English. A large proportion of the educational software produced in the world market is in English. For developing countries in the Asia-Pacific where English language proficiency is not high, especially outside metropolitan areas, this poses a serious barrier in maximizing the educational benefits of the World Wide Web. Even in countries such as Philippines, Malaysia, Singapore, and India where English is the second language; it is desirable that teaching and learning materials, preferably be developed in the local languages.

C. Teachers with ICT Skills

Lack of teachers equipped with ICT skills is another problem for the use of ICT in education. The institutes where ICT is going to be integrated in education, first of all their teachers must be well trained in ICT tools in education. Before going to teach students, teachers must know about how and when to use ICT tools to achieve particular purposes.

D. Change Management

Managing the change is one of the biggest problems, as teachers don't want to accept change easily. Change management issues must be addressed as new work practices, new ways of processing and performing tasks are introduced. In general a large number of teachers in educational institutes are non ICT proficient, and resistance to change. Research has shown that the strategy of adding technology to the already existing activities in institutes and in the classroom, withcut changing habitual teaching practices, does not produce good results in student learning. The reason for this is due to the fact that the vast majority of teachers are not proficient users of technology, especially computer technology. A number of studies have shown that most teachers consider the two main obstacles to using technology in pedagogical practices to be a lack of resources and training.

E. Leadership

Integrating ICT in education is not an easy task, as it requires a wide range of support including higher management, and teachers. Therefore it is necessary to properly convince them for their support, and for this task a leader is required. Leadership is necessary before, during and after project implementation. Before the project is initiated, leadership is needed in order to explain the model, the concept and create awareness; during the project, leadership is needed to manage change and support the project; and after the project, it is needed to pledge the required adaptability and flexibility of the initiative.

Let's conclude, the present age is the age of technology, whereby technology plays a key role in daily lives; this also includes the education system. There are endless possibilities with the integration of ICT in the education system. The use of ICT in education not only improves classroom teaching learning process, but also provides the facility of e-learning. E-learning has rendered convenience of online learning to thousands of learners who cannot avail the benefits of higher education due to several constraints, such as, time, cost, geographical location, age, etc. ICT has enhanced distance learning. The teaching community is able to reach remote areas and learners are able to access qualitative learning environment from anywhere and at anytime. It is important that teachers or trainers should be made to adopt technology in their teaching styles to provide pedagogical and educational gains to the learners.

MODEL QUESTIONS

1. What you mean by blended learning? What are its various forms?
2. What are the opportunities of Integrating ICTs in Education?
3. What are the challenges in Integrating ICTs in Education?

REFERENCES

1. http://derekstockley.com.au/elearning-definition
2. http://en.wikipedia.org/wiki/Education
3. http://en.wikipedia.org/wiki/E-learning

4. http://lyon.chin.gc.ca/.../module3
5. http://searchciomidmarket.techtarget.com/sDefinition/0,,sid183_gci928405,00. html
6. http://www.educ.utas.edu.au/.../thesis/html/design
7. http://www.htk.tlu.ee/TLG/strategy/masterplan2
8. http://www.webopedia.com/TERM/d/distance_learning
9. Proceedings of World Academy of Science, Engineering and Technology Volume 30 July 2008.
10. Pwaset Volume 30 July 2008, waset.org
11. Raju Kumar, http://www.waset.org/pwaset

14
ICT and Distance Education

Distance education, or *distance learning,* is a field of education that focuses on the pedagogy, technology, and instructional systems design that aim to deliver education to students who are not physically "on site." Rather than attending courses in person, teachers and students may communicate at times of their own choosing by exchanging printed or electronic media, or through technology that allows them to communicate in real time and through other online ways. Distance education courses that require a physical on-site presence for any reason including the taking of examinations is considered to be a hybrid or blended course of study.

History

Distance education dates back to at least as early as 1728, when "an advertisement in the Boston Gazette...[named] 'Caleb Phillips, Teacher of the new method of Short Hand" was seeking students for lessons to be sent weekly. Modern distance education has been practiced at least since Isaac Pitman taught shorthand in Great Britain via correspondence in the 1840s. The development of the postal service in the 19th century led to the growth of Commercial Correspondence Colleges with nation-wide reach.

The University of London was the first university to offer distance learning degrees, establishing its External Programme in 1858. The Society to Encourage Studies at Home was founded in 1873 in Boston, Massachusetts. In Australia, the University of Queensland established its Department of Correspondence Studies in 1911. Another pioneering institution was the University of South Africa, which has been offering Correspondence Education courses since

1946. In New Zealand, university-level distance education or extramural study began in 1960 at Massey University. The largest distance education university in the United Kingdom is the *Open University* founded 1969. In Germany the FernUniversität in Hagen was founded 1974. There are now many similar institutions around the world, often with the name *Open University* and more than a dozen of them have grown to become 'mega-universities', a term coined to denote institutions with more than 100,000 students.

Charles Wedemeyer of the University of Wisconsin at Madison is considered the father of modern distance education in America. From 1964-68 the Carnegie Foundation funded Wedemeyer's *Articulated Instructional Media Project* (AIM) which brought in a variety of communications technologies aimed at providing learning to an off-campus population. According to Moore's recounting, AIM impressed the British who imported these ideas and used them to create the first Open University, now called United Kingdom Open University (UKOU) to distinguish it from other open universities which have emerged. UKOU was established in the late 1960s and used television and radio as its primary delivery methodologies, thus placing it in the forefront of applying emerging technologies to learning. It is fair to say that all "open universities" use distance education technologies as delivery methodologies. There are many private and public, non-profit and for-profit institutions offering courses and degree programmes through distance education. Levels of accreditation vary; some institutions offering distance education in the United States have received little outside oversight, and some may be fraudulent diploma mills. In many other jurisdictions, an institution may not use the term "University" without accreditation and authorisation, normally by the National Government. Online education is rapidly increasing among mainstream universities in the United States, where online doctoral programmes have even developed at prestigious research institutions.

In the twentieth century, radio, television, and the Internet have all been used to further distance education. Computers and the Internet have made distance learning distribution easier and faster. Private, for-profit Phoenix University, which is primarily an online university, now has two hundred thousand students and expects to serve five hundred thousand by 2010, yet little is known about student success or lack of success in such a fast-growing institution. In 2006 the Sloan Consortium reported that more than 96 per cent of the largest colleges and universities in the United States offered online courses and that almost 3.2 million U.S. students were taking at least one online course during the fall 2005 term.

One of Canada's leading distance education providers is Open Learning (TRU-OL) of Thompson Rivers University. TRU-OL educational goals are obtainable for anyone through accessible and varied courses that can be taken anytime and at an individually-determined pace. With over 400 individual courses and more than 57 programmes available for completion by distance and online learning, students can take a variety of programmes such as: Adult secondary school completion; certificates and diplomas, including advanced and post-baccalaureate; associate degrees; and bachelor's degrees.

In Ontario, Canada the Ministry of Training, Colleges and Universities established the elearnnetwork.ca in 2007 to provide access to students in small and rural communities across Ontario who wanted to pursue college or university courses from their community by distance education.

In the province of Manitoba, the Department of Education, Citizenship and Youth provides three options in distance education: Independent Study Option, Teacher Mediated Option and Web-based Course Option.

The Independent Study Option (ISO) provides the opportunity and flexibility for both school-age and adult learners to study a wide range of compulsory optional print based distance education courses from Grades 7 to 12. This form of distance education also provides students with support by e-mail or phone. The Independent Study Option also offers several courses in French. In the event that a student leaves the province on a temporary or permanent basis, the ISO also provides the opportunity for continuing the study of Manitoba curriculum en route to receiving a Senior Years graduation diploma.

Teacher Mediated Option (TMO) supports the delivery of distance learning courses that are scheduled within the school day and use a variety of technologies to assist students including: Instruction twice a school cycle for 40 minutes per class by audio teleconference, recording of classes as required for use up to five days after the class has occurred, and corresponding with an instructor between classes by e-mail or phone. These courses are only available to students attending school or an adult learning centre.

Web-bases course in Manitoba are available to schools wishing to deliver high school courses on the internet. Manitoba uses the Blackboard learning System CE version 6.2. While being delivered through the internet, these courses are taught by a teacher who may be off-site. Assignments are submitted online by students to teachers, and a final examination is written on site.

Technologies Used in Delivery

The types of available technologies used in distance education are divided into two groups: *Synchronous* and *asynchronous*. Synchronous technology is a mode of online delivery where all participants are "present" at the same time. Requires a timetable to be organized. Asynchronous technology is a mode of online delivery where participants access course materials on their own schedule. Students are not required to be together at the same time.

Synchronous Technologies

- Telephone
- Videoconferencing
- Web Conferencing.

Asynchronous Technologies

- Audiocassette
- E-mail
- Message Board Forums
- Social Learning websites (social networking sites that focus on e-learning)
- Print Materials
- Voice Mail/Fax
- Videocassette.

There are also Learning Management Systems or Learning Management Content Systems which can be used for both Synchronous and Asynchronous learning. (LMS is not so much a learning tool as a framework for an instructor to better administer the classroom).

Types of Distance Education Courses

- Correspondence conducted through regular mail
- Internet conducted either synchronously or asynchronously

- Telecourse/Broadcast, in which content is delivered via radio or television
- CD-ROM, in which the student interacts with computer content stored on a CD-ROM
- PocketPC/Mobile Learning where the student accesses course content stored on a mobile device or through a wireless server
- Integrated distance learning, the integration of live, in-group instruction or interaction with a distance learning curriculum.

Distance Education has traversed four to five 'generations' of technology in its history. These are print, audio/video broadcasting, audio/video teleconferencing, computer aided instruction, e-learning/online-learning, computer broadcasting/webcasting etc. Yet the radio remains a very viable form, especially in the developing nations, because of its reach. In India the FM Channel is very popular and is being used by universities, to broadcast educational programmes of variety on areas such as teacher education, rural development, programmes in agriculture for farmers, science education, creative writing, mass communication, in addition to traditional courses in liberal arts, science and business administration. The increasing popularity of MP3 players, PDAs and Smart Phone has provided an additional medium for the distribution of distance education content, and some professors now allow students to listen or even watch video of a course as a Podcast. Some colleges have been working with the U.S. military to distribute entire course content on a PDA to deployed personnel.

Testing and Evaluation

Distance education has long had trouble with testing. The delivery of testing materials is fairly straightforward, which makes sure it is available to the student and he or she can read it at their leisure. The problem arises when the student is required to complete assignments and testing. Online courses have had difficulty controlling cheating in quizzes, tests, or examinations because of the lack of teacher control. In a classroom situation a teacher can monitor students and visually uphold a level of integrity consistent with an institution's reputation. However, with distance education the student can be removed from supervision completely. Some schools address integrity issues concerning testing by requiring students to take examinations in a controlled setting.

Assignments have adapted by becoming larger, longer, and more thorough so as to test for knowledge by forcing the student to research the subject and prove they have done the work. Quizzes are a popular form of testing knowledge and many courses go by the honour system regarding cheating. Even if the student is checking questions in the textbook or online, there may be an enforced time limit or the quiz may be worth so little in the overall mark that it becomes inconsequential. Exams and bigger tests may be harder to regulate.

Used in combination with invigilators, a pre-arranged supervisor trusted with overseeing big tests and examinations may be used to increase security. Many Midterms and Final examinations are held at a common location so that professors can supervise directly. When the Internet became a popular medium for distance education many websites were founded offering secure exam software and packages to help professors manage their students more effectively.

MODEL QUESTIONS

1. How ICT promoting Distance Education?
2. What are the technologies used in delivery of distance learning material?
3. What are the types of distance education courses?

REFERENCES

1. "Key Facts", University of London External Programme Website, http://www.londonexternal.ac.uk/about_us/facts.
2. Daniel, J.S. (1996). *Mega-Universities and Knowledge Media: Technology Strategies for Higher Education*, Kogan Page, London.
3. Hebert, D.G. (2007). "Five Challenges and Solutions in Online Music Teacher Education," Research and Issues in Music Education, Vol. 5.
4. Holmberg, B. (2005). *The Evolution, Principles and Practices of Distance Education.* Bibliotheks-und Informations system der Universitat Oldenburg.
5. http://en.wikipedia.org/wiki/Distance_education
6. Moore, Michael G.; Greg Kearsley (2005). *Distance Education: A Systems View*, Second, Belmont, CA: Wadsworth.
7. White, M. (1982). 'Distance Education in Australian Higher Education— A History', *Distance Education*, Vol. 3, Issue 2.

15

ICTs and Teacher Education: Global Context and Framework

Information and Communication Technologies (ICTs) are a major factor in shaping the new global economy and producing rapid changes in society. Within the past decade, the new ICT tools have fundamentally changed the way people communicate and do business. They have produced significant transformations in industry, agriculture, medicine, business, engineering and other fields. They also have the potential to transform the nature of education-where and how learning takes place and the roles of students and teachers in the learning process.

Teacher education institutions may either assume a leadership role in the transformation of education or be left behind in the swirl of rapid technological change. For education to reap the full benefits of ICTs in learning, it is essential that pre-service and in-service teachers have basic ICT skills and competencies. Teacher education institutions and programmes must provide the leadership for pre-service and in-service teachers and model the new pedagogies and tools for learning. They must also provide leadership in determining how the new technologies can best be used in the context of the culture, needs, and economic conditions within their country.

To accomplish these goals, teacher education institutions must work closely and effectively with K-12 teachers and administrators, national or state educational agencies, teacher unions, business and community organizations, politicians and other important stateholders in the educational system. Teacher education institutions also need to develop strategies and plans to enhance the teaching-learning process within teacher education programmes and to assure that all future teachers are well prepared to use the new tools for learning.

Global Context

As noted in the UNESCO World Education Report, *Teachers and Teaching in a Changing World* (UNESCO, 1998), the young generation is entering a world that is changing in all spheres: Scientific and technological, political, economic, social, and cultural. The emergence of the 'knowledge-based' society is changing the global economy and the status of education.

There is growing awareness among policy-makers, business leaders and educators that the educational system designed to prepare learners for an agrarian or industrially-based economy will not provide students with the knowledge and skills they will need to thrive in the 21st century's knowledge-based economy and society. The new knowledge-based global society is one in which:

- the world's knowledge base doubles every 2–3 years;
- 7,000 scientific and technical articles are published each day;
- data sent from satellites orbiting the earth transmit enough data to fill 19 million volumes every two weeks.

ICTs in Teacher Education

These new possibilities exist largely as the result of two converging forces. First the quantity of information available in the world-much of it relevant to survival and basic well-being-is exponentially greater than that available only a few years ago, and the rate of its growth is accelerating. A synergistic effect occurs when important information is coupled with a second modern advance-the new capacity to communicate among people of the world. The opportunity exists to harness this force and use it positively, consciously, and with design, in order to contribute to meeting defined learning needs. As is the case for other sectors of the wider economy and society, education will need to come to terms with the new technologies. This could require substantial public and private sector investments in software research and development, purchase of hardware, and refurnishment of schools. It will be difficult for national policy-makers to resist finding the necessary resources, whatever their sensibilities for expenditure on education, although without international co-operation and assistance the poorest countries could fall still further behind. Parents and the public at large, in the industrial countries at least, are unlikely to accept for too long the notion that education should be less well equipped with the new technologies than other areas of social and economic activity (UNESCO World Education Report, 1998, pp. 19-20).

- graduates of secondary schools in industrialized nations have been exposed to more information than their grandparents were in a lifetime;
- there will be as much change in the next three decades as there was in the last three centuries (National School Board Association, 2002).

The challenge confronting our educational systems is how to transform the curriculum and teaching-learning process to provide students with the skills to function effectively in this dynamic, information-rich, and continuously changing environment. The technology-based global economy also poses challenges to countries as national economies become more internationalized, with the increasing flow of information, technology, products, capital, and people between nations. This new economic environment is creating a new era of global competition for goods, services, and expertise. All of these changes are producing dramatic shifts in the political, economic and social structures of many countries around the world. In industrialized nations, the economic base is shifting from industry to information. This shift also demands new knowledge and skills in the work force.

ICTs have changed the nature of work and the types of skills needed in most fields and professions. While they have, on the one hand, created a wide array of new jobs, many of which did not even exist ten years ago, they have also replaced the need for many types of unskilled or low-skilled workers. For example, the new 'smart' agricultural equipment, using advance digital and industrial technology, is able to do the work previously done with a large number of low-skilled agricultural workers. In addition, new manufacturing plants are requiring fewer low-skilled workers. A Canadian study notes, for example, that in high-tech companies only 10 per cent of the work force is comprised of unskilled workers (National School Board Association, 2002). These trends pose new challenges to educational systems to prepare students with the knowledge and skills needed to thrive in a new and dynamic environment of continuous technological change and accelerating growth in knowledge production.

Education is at the confluence of powerful and rapidly shifting educational, technological and political forces that will shape the structure of educational systems across the globe for the remainder of this century. Many countries are engaged in a number of efforts to effect changes in the teaching/learning process to prepare students for an information and technology based society. The UNESCO World Education Report (1998) notes that the new technologies challenge traditional conceptions of both teaching and learning and, by reconfiguring how teachers and learners gain access to knowledge, have the potential to transform teaching and learning processes. ICTs provide an array of powerful tools that may help in transforming the present isolated, teacher-centred and text-bound classrooms into rich, student-focused, interactive knowledge environments. To meet these challenges, schools must embrace the new technologies and appropriate the new ICT tools for learning. They must also move toward the goal of transforming the traditional paradigm of learning. To accomplish this goal requires both a change in the traditional view of the learning process and an understanding of how the new digital technologies can create new learning environments in which students are engaged learners, able to take greater responsibility for their own learning and constructing their own knowledge. Thomas Kuhn suggests that revolutions in science come about when the old theories and methods will not solve new problems. He calls these changes in theory and methods a "paradigm shift." There is widespread concern that the educational experiences provided in many schools will not prepare students well for the future. Many educators and business and government leaders believe that creating a paradigm shift in views of the learning process, coupled with applications of the new information technologies, may play an important role in bringing educational systems into alignment with the knowledge-based, information-rich society.

The Traditional View of the Learning Process

The existing view of the learning process emerged out of the factory model of education at the turn of the 20th century and was highly effective in preparing large numbers of individuals with skills needed for low-skilled positions in industry and agriculture. The innovation of classrooms with 20-30 students was created along with the concept of standardized instruction for everyone. In the traditional, teacher-centred approach to learning the teacher is the expert and the dispenser of knowledge to the students. It is largely a 'broadcast' model of learning where the teacher serves as the repository and transmitter of knowledge to the students. The traditional educational paradigm is often characterized by the following views of learning:

- *Learning is hard:* Many view learning as a difficult and often tedious process. According to this view, if students are having fun or enjoying what they are doing in a learning activity, they probably are not learning.
- *Learning is based on a deficit model of the student:* The system strives to identify deficiencies and weaknesses of the student. Based on noted deficiencies, students are tracked, categorized, remediated or failed. The impact of the deficit model of student learning is most obvious in compensatory education programmes. As implied by the term, compensatory education is designed to make up or remediate learning that some children, particularly poor minority children, do not have, but which the curriculum and structure of schooling assume are common to all children.

Bruer, in his book, *Schools for Thought,* notes that research overwhelmingly concentrates on the weaknesses of poor children. Very little research has been done on their strengths. In addition, the weaknesses identified are often deficiencies in terms of the traditional organization and content of schooling. Very little thought has been given to the idea of changing schooling to accommodate new kinds of students; all the effort has gone to changing the students so that they will fit into the schools. In addition, the underlying assumptions about poor students' motivation, language, and conceptual development have..."militated against offering them a literacy of thoughtfulness and have favoured a low-level, atomized, concrete, basic-skills curriculum. The language of that curriculum has been so simplified that it is both boring and artificial. It has been stripped of its richness and context and made fundamentally meaningless, which is to say unabsorbable by normal people, except through memorization, whose effects last only a few hours or days." (Bruer, 1993).

- *Learning is a process of information transfer and reception:* Much of our present learning enterprise remains "information-oriented," emphasizing students *reproducing knowledge* rather than *producing their own knowledge.* It also remains teacher-centred. Many still see the role of the teacher as a dispenser of information and the role of the student as a passive receiver, storer and repeater of the transmitted information. The prevalence of this view is supported by observations that teachers continue to rely on old standbys such as lectures, textbook reading, and fill-in-the-worksheets practices that reduce students to passive recipients of information and fail to develop their thinking skills.

- *Learning is an individual/solitary process:* In a study of schools in the United States, the National Assessment of Educational Progress noted that most students spend long hours working alone at their desks completing worksheets or repetitive tasks. A London Times survey of English school children indicated that students almost unanimously rejected this daily ordeal of dull and ritualistically solitary classroom activity and called for a broader and more exciting curriculum. Above all, they wanted more work allowing them to *think for themselves*. They wanted to design and make things, to experiment and to engage in first-hand observation. The Times reported, however, that there was little evidence of changes in the curriculum that would respond to the students' wishes. (Resta, 1996)
- *Learning is facilitated by breaking content/instruction into small isolated units*: The educational system is often geared more to categorizing and analyzing patches of knowledge than to sewing them together.

  Bruer (1993) notes that the technology of mass education is quite adept at "breaking knowledge and skills into thousands of little standardized, decontextualized pieces, which could be taught and tested one at a time."

  Neil Postman in his book, *Teaching as a Subversive Activity*, states that our educational systems break knowledge and experience into "subjects, relentlessly turning wholes into parts, history into events without restoring continuity." (Postman, 1969).
- *Learning is a linear process*: Frequently, the textbook or teacher provides only one linear path through a narrowly bounded content area or sequence of standardized instructional units. For example, in a mathematics text only one correct problem

solution trail may be offered for a specific subclass of problems. However, the problems encountered in daily life (or in mathematics) seldom have only one solution path or sequence.

Changes in Views of the Learning Process

In contrast to the traditional teaching-learning paradigm, a new paradigm of the teaching-learning process is emerging, based on three decades of research in human learning, that encompasses the following views of the human learning process:

- *Learning is a natural process*: The natural state of the brain is to learn, however, not everyone learns in the same way. There are different learning, perceptual and personality styles that must be considered in the design of learning experiences for the individual student. Given interesting and rich learning environments, and supportive and stimulating teachers, students will learn. Teachers have often noted that children who appear disruptive or to have short attention spans when confronted with typical classroom instruction, may spend long periods engaged in meaningful and interesting computer-related activities.
- *Learning is a social process*: The communal context of knowledge and learning is beginning to be rediscovered, as evidenced by the rapid growth of quality circles and computer-supported collaborative work in business, government, medicine, and higher education. As Vygotsky (1978) noted long ago, students learn best in collaboration with peers, teachers, parents, and others when they are actively engaged in meaningful, interesting tasks. ICTs provide opportunities for teachers and students to collaborate with others across the country and across the globe. They also provide new tools to support this collaborative learning in the classroom and online.
- *Learning is an active and not a passive process*: In most fields, people are faced with the challenge of *producing knowledge* rather than simply *reproducing knowledge*. To allow students to move toward competence, they must be actively engaged in the learning process, in activities such as solving real problems, producing original writing, completing scientific research projects (rather than simply studying about science),

dialoguing with others on important issues, providing artistic and musical performances, and constructing physical objects. The traditional curriculum asks students only to recall and describe what others have accomplished or produced. While all production of knowledge must be based on an understanding of prior knowledge, the mère reproduction of knowledge, without its connection to the production of knowledge, is largely a passive activity that neither fully engages nor challenges the student.

- *Learning may either be linear or non-linear:*Much of what now hapens in schools appears based on the notion that the mind works like a serial processor that is designed to process only one piece of information at a time in sequential order. But the mind is a wonderful parallel processor that may attend to and process many different types of information simultaneously. Cognitive theory and research sees learning as a reorganization of knowledge structures. The knowledge structures are stored in semantic memory as schema or cognitive maps. Students "learn" by augmenting, combining, and rearranging a collection of cognitive maps, many of which overlap or are interconnected through a complex network of associations. There are many ways that students may acquire and process information and assimilate it into their existing knowledge structures. Although some knowledge domains, such as mathematics, may perhaps lend themselves to a linear approach, not all learning can or should occur linearly.
- *Learning is integrative and contextualized*: Pribram's holistic brain theory suggests that information presented globally is more easily assimilated than information presented only in a sequence of information elements (Pribram, 1991). It is also easier for students to see relations and to make connections. Jacob Bronowski (1990), in *Science and Human Values*, made the point that to discover the connection between what had seemed two isolated facts of existence is a creative act, whether the field is art or science. He calls it an act of unifying. This is not something that can be done for learners; these connections cannot be made in learners' minds. Information can be given, the connection can even be stated. But even if the information is repeated, it cannot be assumed it is really

known. The learners must discover it for themselves. That is not to say that learners must discover everything unaided. The teacher's role is to help them in several ways to make connections and to integrate knowledge.

- *Learning is based on a strength model of student abilities, interest, and culture*: Based on the work of Howard Gardner and others, schools are beginning to consider the specific strengths and interests that students bring to the learning environment, and are designing learning activities that build on student strengths rather than focusing only upon remediating weaknesses. In addition, schools increasingly recognize diversity as a resource rather than a problem in the classroom. In contrast to the remedial and standardized concept of instruction, diversity and individual differences are valued and the learning process is designed to build on the strengths and assets brought by the learner to the classroom.
- *Learning is assessed through task completion, products, and real problem solving of both individual and group efforts*: Rather than simply evaluating students through paper and pencil tests, assessments are made using portfolios of actual performances and work in both collaborative and individual learning tasks. The traditional view of the learning process is typically teacher-centred, with teachers doing most of the talking and intellectual work, while students are passive receptacles of the information provided. This is not to indicate that the traditional lecture method is without value, as it allows the teacher to quickly convey lots of information to students and is a useful strategy for recall or rote learning. However, it is not the most effective way to help students develop and use higher order cognitive skills to solve complex real world problems. As noted by Driscoll (1994), we no longer can view learners as "empty vessels waiting to be filled, but rather as active organisms seeking meaning."

Don Tapscott, in his book *Growing Up Digital: The Rise of the Next Generation* (1998), notes that we are entering a new era of digital learning in which we are in the process of transitioning from "broadcast" learning to "interactive" learning. Today's students no longer want to be passive recipients in the information transfer model of learning. Rather they want to be active participants in the learning process. There is growing recognition that today's world requires that students be able to work collaboratively with others, think critically and creatively, and reflect on their own learning processes.

A Shift from Teaching to Learning

As technology has created change in all aspects of society, it is also changing our expectations of what students must learn in order to function in the new world economy. Students will have to learn to navigate through large amounts of information, to analyze and make decisions, and to master new knowledge domains in an increasingly technological society. They will need to be lifelong learners, collaborating with others in accomplishing complex tasks, and effectively using different systems for representing and communicating knowledge to others. A shift from teacher-centred instruction to learner-centred instruction is needed to enable students to acquire the new 21st century knowledge and skills.

Shifting the emphasis from teaching to learning can create a more interactive and engaging learning environment for teachers and learners. This new environment also involves a change in the roles of both teachers and students. The role of the teacher will change from knowledge transmitter to that of learning facilitator, knowledge guide, knowledge navigator and co-learner with the student. The new role does not diminish the importance of the teacher but requires new knowledge and skills. Students will have greater responsibility for their own learning in this environment as they seek out, find, synthesize, and share their knowledge with others. ICTs provide powerful tools to support the shift to student-centred learning and the new roles of teachers and students.

Theories Supporting the New View of the Learning Process

The new views of the learning process and the shift to student-centred learning have emerged based on cognitive learning research and the confluence of several theories that have informed our understanding of the nature and context of learning. Some of the most prominent theories include: Socio-cultural theory (based on Vygotsky's intersubjectiveness and Zone of Proximal Development), constructivism theory, self-regulated learning, situated cognition, cognitive apprenticeship, problem-based learning (Cognition and Technology Group at Vanderbilt), cognitive flexibility theory (Spiro *et al.*, 1988), and distributed cognition (Salomon *et al.*, 1993). Each of these theories is based on the same underlying assumptions that learners are active agents, purposefully seeking and constructing knowledge within a meaningful context. The learning environment that may be derived from this view of the learning Process. The student-centred environment shows that the learner interacts with other students, the teacher, information resources, and technology. The learner engages in authentic tasks in authentic contexts using authentic tools and is assessed through authentic performance. The environment provides the learner with coaching and scaffolding in developing knowledge and skills. It provides a rich collaborative environment enabling the learner to consider diverse and multiple perspectives to address issues and solve problems. It also provides opportunities for the student to reflect on his or her learning. Although the new learning environment can be created without the use of technology, it is clear that ICTs can provide powerful tools to help learners access vast knowledge resources, collaborate with others, consult with experts, share knowledge, and solve complex problems using cognitive tools. ICTs also provide learners with powerful new tools to represent their knowledge with text, images, graphics, and video.

The new view of the learning process is based on research that has emerged from theoretical frameworks related to human learning. Many reflect a constructivism view of the learning process. In this view, learners are active agents who engage in their own knowledge construction by integrating new information into their schema or mental structures. The learning process is seen as a process of "meaning-making" in socially, culturally, historically, and politically situated contexts. In a constructivism learning environment, students construct their own knowledge by testing ideas and approaches based on their prior knowledge and experience, applying these to new tasks, contexts and situations, and integrating the new knowledge gained with pre-existing intellectual constructs.

A constructivist environment involves developing learning communities comprised of students, teachers and experts who are engaged in authentic tasks in authentic contexts closely related to work done in the real world. A constructivist learning environment also provides opportunities for learners to experience multiple perspectives. Through discussion or debate, learners are able to see issues and problems from different points of view, to negotiate meaning, and develop shared understandings with others. The constructivist learning environment also emphasizes authentic assessment of learning rather than the traditional paper/pencil test. Some of the most influential theories that relate to new views of the learning process include:

Vygotsky's Socio-cultural Theory

Vygotsky's socio-cultural theory of human learning describes learning as a social process and the origination of human intelligence in society or culture. The major theme of Vygotsky's theoretical framework is that social interaction plays a fundamental role in the development of cognition. Vygotsky believed everything is learned on two levels. First, through interaction with others, and then integrated into the individual's mental structure.

ICTs and Teacher Education

Every function in the child's cultural development appears twice: First, on the social level, and later, on the individual level; first, between people (interpsychological) and then inside the child (intrapsychological). This applies equally to voluntary attention, to logical memory, and to the formation of concepts. All the higher functions originate as actual relationships between individuals. (Vygotsky, 1978, p. 57).

A second aspect of Vygotsky's theory is the idea that the potential for cognitive development is limited to a "Zone of Proximal Development" (ZPD). This "zone" is the area of exploration for which the student is cognitively prepared, but requires help and social interaction to fully develop (Briner, 1999). A teacher or more experienced peer is able to provide the learner with "scaffolding" to support the student's evolving understanding of knowledge domains or development of complex skills. Collaborative learning, discourse, modelling, and scaffolding are strategies for supporting the intellectual knowledge and skills of learners and facilitating intentional learning. The implications of Vygotsky theory are that learners should be provided with socially rich environments in which to explore knowledge domains with their fellow students, teachers and outside experts. ICTs can be used to support the learning environment by providing tools for discourse, discussions, collaborative writing, and problem-solving, and by providing online support systems to scaffold students evolving understanding and cognitive growth.

Jean Piaget

Based on his research on the development of children's cognitive functions, Piaget's work is regarded by many as the founding principles of constructivist theory. He observed that learning occurs through adaptation to interactions with the environment. Disequilibrium (mental conflict which demands resolution) gives rise to Assimilation of a new experience, which is added to the existing knowledge of the learner, or to Accommodation, which is modification of existing understanding to provide for the new experience. Specifically, Piaget posited that the existing cognitive structures of the learner determine how new information is perceived and processed. If the new information makes sense to the existing mental structure of the learner, then the new information item is incorporated into the structure (i.e., Assimilation). If, however, the data are very different from the existing mental structure of the learner, they are either rejected or transformed in ways so that it fits into the structure (i.e., Accommodation). The learner has an active role in constructing his or her own knowledge in both of these ideas. He observed that, as children assimilated new information into their existing mental structures, their ideas gained complexity and power, and their understanding of the world grew in richness and depth. These ideas are core concepts of the constructivism view of the learning process. (Jean Piaget Society, 2001).

Jerome Bruner

Similar to Piaget, Bruner emphasized that learning is an active process in which learners construct new ideas or concepts based upon their prior knowledge and experience. He identified three principles to guide the development of instruction. These include: (1) instruction must be concerned with the experiences and contexts that make the student willing and able to learn (readiness); (2) instruction must be structured so that the student can easily grasp it (spiral organization); and, (3) instruction should be designed to facilitate extrapolation and/or fill in the gaps (going beyond the information given).

Problem-Based Learning

The goals of Problem-Based Learning (PBL) are to develop higher order thinking skills by providing students with authentic and complex problems and cases. This approach to learning provides a more authentic context for learning and engages students in authentic tasks. It is used frequently in fields such as engineering, medicine and architecture, and has been increasingly applied to K-12 settings. Through the process of working together, articulating theories, creating hypotheses, and critically discussing the ideas of others, students move to deeper levels of understanding of the problem. The self-directed learning strategies developed in PBL may help foster students' lifelong learning.

Anchored Instruction

Anchored instruction is an approach to designing instruction that is 'anchored' in a real world context, problem or situation. Technology has been used to help create 'real world' contexts and situations through the use of video. The video segments provide the context for the subsequent learning and instruction. (Bransford and Stein, 1993).

Distributed Cognition

Distributed cognition emphasizes that cognitive growth is fostered through interaction with others and involves dialogue and discourse, making private knowledge public and developing shared understandings. Tools for online collaboration have been designed to support collaborative knowledge construction and sharing in the classroom. (Oshima, Bereiter, and Scardamalia, 1995).

Cognitive Flexibility Theory

This theory asserts that people acquire knowledge in ill-structured domains by constructing multiple representations and linkages among knowledge units. It also notes that learners revisit the same concepts and principles in a variety of contexts. The theory is useful in understanding how knowledge is transferred in ill-structured knowledge domains. (Spiro *et al.*, 1988).

Cognitive Apprenticeship

Cognitive apprenticeship is a term for the instructional process in which teachers or more experienced or knowledgeable peers provide 'scaffolds' to support learners' cognitive growth and development. Cognitive apprenticeship permits students to learn through their interactions, construct knowledge, and share knowledge-building experiences with the other members of the learning community. ICTs provide powerful new tools to support cognitive apprenticeships, enabling groups to share online workspaces to collaboratively develop artifacts and intellectual products. They also make possible tele-apprenticeships, in which an expert is able to work with or mentor a student who may be thousands of miles distant.

Situated Learning

Situated learning emphasizes the use of apprenticeship, coaching, collaboration, authentic contexts, tasks, activities and cognitive tools (Brown, Collins and Duguid, 1989). It occurs when students work on authentic tasks that take place in real-world settings (Winn, 1993). Learning is viewed as a function of the activity, context and culture in which it occurs, which contrasts with most classroom learning which is abstract and out of context (Lave, 1988). Situated cognition theory emphasizes providing an authentic context for the learner and encouraging social interaction and collaboration in the learning environment. Through collaborative problem solving, dialogue, and discussion students are able to develop deeper levels of understanding of a problem or knowledge domain.

Self-Regulated Learning

Self-regulated learners are those who are aware of their own knowledge and understandings, i.e., what they know and what they do not know or need to understand. It combines self-observation, self-judgment, and self-reaction. Self-regulation plays a crucial role in all phases of learning and has the potential to increase the meaningfulness of students' classroom learning (Schoenfeld, 1987).

ICT tools can be used to make students' tacit knowledge public and to help them develop metacognitive skills and become more reflective and self-regulated learners (Hsiao, 1999).

These theories that undergird the new views of the learning process help shape the new pedagogies for learning. Ultimately, the power of ICTs will be determined by the ability of teachers to use the new tools for learning to create rich, new, and engaging learning environments for their students. The UNESCO World Education Report (1998) notes that: The challenge for ICTs in Teacher Education is to assure that the new generation of teachers, as well as current teachers, are well prepared to use new learning methods, processes and materials with the new ICT tools for learning. The following sections provide a road map to help teacher education institutions meet the challenge.

MODEL QUESTIONS

1. How ICT affecting Teacher Education? Discuss.

2. What are the changes in the views of Learning Process?
3. What are the theories supporting the new view of the Learning Process.

REFERENCES

1. Jean Piaget Society. 2001. URL: http://www.piaget.org.
2. Khvilon, E. & Patru, M. (2002). Information & Communication Technologies in Teacher Education, A Planning Guide, UNESCO Division of Higher Education.
3. Lave, J. 1988. Cognition in Practice: Mind, Mathematics, and Culture in Everyday Life. Cambridge, UK: Cambridge University Press. In Lave, J., & Wenger, E. 1990. *Situated Learning: Legitimate Peripheral Participation*. Cambridge, UK: Cambridge University Press.
4. Newby, T., Stepich, D., Lehman, J., and Russel, J. 2000. *Instructional Technology for Teaching and Learning*. Upper Saddle River, Merrill/ Prentice Hall, New Jersey: National School Board Association. 2002. *Why Change?*: http://www.nsba.org/sbot/toolkit/WhyChange.html
5. Oshima, J., Bereiter, C., and Scardamalia, M. 1995. Information-Access Characteristics for High Conceptual Progress in a Computer-Networked Learning Environment. In *Proceedings CSCL'95 (Computer Support for Collaborative Learning) Conference.*
6. Postman, N. 1969. *Teaching as a Subversive Activity*. Doubleday, New York.
7. Pribram, K. 1991. *Brain and Perception: Holonomy and Structure in Figural Processing Lawrence Erlbaum*, Mahwah, New Jersey.
8. Resta, P. 1996. *Technology and Changing Views of the Learning Process*. Texas School Boards Association Journal, 11 (8).
9. Salomon, G. (Ed.). 1993. *Distributed Cognitions: Psychological and Educational Considerations*. Cambridge University Press.

16
National Policy on ICT in School Education

Capacity Building of Schools and Teachers in ICT

The critical factor in the successful integration of ICT into teacher education is the extent to which the teacher educators have the knowledge and skills in ICT integration. A well-conceived and sustained programme of professional development is therefore required to enable the teacher educators and master teachers to develop these skills. This may require development and revision of existing teacher training curriculum guidelines for pre-service and in-service teachers. This brings to the front some of the very pertinent questions like:

- What are the methods of skilling and re-skilling educators to adapt and to adopt to the changing faces of technology?
- How can educators be guided on effective use of these new tools that focus on learning activities, rather than content delivery or general learner management?
- How to build buy-in and ownership among educators and motivate them to spearhead the ICT-based education process?

In order to find out appropriate answers on these above questions which can be suggested for the formulation of the Indian National Policy on ICT in School Education, Global eSchools and Communities Initiative (GeSCI) along with Centre for Science, Development and Media Studies (CSDMS) as a core facilitating partner organised a national level Round Table discussion and consultation on Capacity Building of Schools and Teachers in ICT under the aegis of Ministry of HRD, Government of India, in New Delhi on September 30, 2008.

Digital Learning Team of CSDMS captures the proceedings, discussions, and recommendations of the capacity building session of schools and teachers in ICT.

The discussions in the Round Table revolved around the questions mentioned above where the participants exchanged their views and expert comments and tried to reach at compiling some guidelines and recommendation points for the purpose of drafting the ICT policy in school education.

Shri Arun Kumar Rath, Secretary, Department of School Education & Literacy, Ministry of Human Resource Development suggested to address a broader set of issues related to teachers' recruitment and training in a time bound manner.

Shri S.C. Khuntia, Joint Secretary, Department of School Education and Literacy, MHRD expected that the forthcoming policy on ICT in school education will address various issues related to capacity building adequately. He felt, with enhanced use of ICTs, school education will make a paradigm shift.

Prof. Mohd. Akhtar Siddiqui, Chairman, National Council for Teacher Education (NCTE), highlighted in his talk the need for continuous capacity building of teachers. He informed that NCTE has initiated the process of developing a draft National Policy on Teacher Education.

Mr. Pulkkinen shared the global vision and GeSCI's experience on providing guidelines on effective capacity building mechanisms for teachers and schools in several countries. He urged for developing an understanding and consensus on role of ICT in education and skills required by the teachers.

The participants were engaged in intensive discussion on various critical issues related to capacity building of teachers and schools and raising several pertinent questions. Participants shared different perspectives, experiences and feedback. The discussion led to a better understanding on the issues related to professional development of educators on integrating ICTs in the teaching and learning processes. A set of recommendations emerged out of the discussion.

Annie Koshi, Principal of St. Mary's School suggested the need to define the objective of education and role of ICTs in education. It was argued that different levels of education require different sets of action and strategy. The need was felt for understanding the skills required by teachers for integrating ICTs in education and was reiterated by Dr. Anjlee Prakash, CEO, Learning Links Foundation.

The participants urged to deal with the issues of motivation and morale also. The need was felt to enhance the role and participation of State Government Agencies and Institutions like State Council Educational Research and Training. Post training follow up with the teachers and providing one laptop per teacher was recommended by Dr. S.N. Uma of NIIT. The group discussed that all school teachers should be skilled and re-skilled from time to time with content available in local languages. Vineeta Dixit, CEO of SW applications emphasised that digital divide is about access to and familiarity with technology. A teacher friendly software is required for training teachers in using information and communication technology. There is a lack of infrastructure and capacity to optimise the ICT tools to achieve educational objectives. Dr. Prabhjot Kaur, Principal M.V. College of Education suggested that B.Ed. courses should include and increase ICT in Teacher Training. There is a need to allow space and flexibility for the teachers to discover and explore the possibilities of integrating ICT in education. Prof. Marmar Mukhopadhyay, Director, Educational Technology Management Academy also brought up to the group that there should be a model based on case studies of teacher training across the country. There should be effort to build and bind motivation for training of the teahers in education process. Some pertinent points were raised by Prof. M.M. Pant, Former Pro Vice-Chancellor, IGNOU who reiterated that there is a need to develop mechanism of teacher training and delivery of interactive content; sharing e-Content and sharing experience in web 2.0, emphasising learning over content delivery and metrics of learning as a process.

Discussion also covered the issues of training, content, language, infrastructure, access, educational management and monitoring and evaluation.

Recommendations

The Teacher training curriculum in the country does not acknowledge the new age environment in schools and classrooms. There is a wide gap between the curriculum taught to teacher educators and the reality that exists in schools. With the exception of a miniscule percentage of well equipped schools, all the other schools are grappling with chronic issues of proper school buildings, teaching materials, shortage of teachers, absenteeism of teachers, severe drop out rates of children, lack of proper sanitation and drinking water facilities are just a few of the problems. The teachers in our government schools play multifarious roles; trying to deal with these issues and several others. In such a situation, we have a new pressure point and that is introducing ICTs in the school. Teachers technically trained on traditional methods of lesson delivery cannot be suddenly expected to turn into technology wizards and churn out lessons by the hour. This needs a well thought out plan of action on skilling and re-skilling teachers across the country and has to be continuous.

A. The issues therefore are not of training or capacity building in the regular sense, but that of teacher empowerment. This requires that existing teacher training curriculum be modified to match the efforts made by the ministry to set up technology enabled environments in schools. Therefore, teacher training curriculum for government and private colleges should undergo a mandatory change with immediate effect. NCTE can take a lead in providing direction on this.

B. In Service teachers need to be introduced to technology tools, so that they may be able to use them easily. This will require regular training. There is a need for regular skilling of teachers: On using ICT resources to create and manage a learning environment, training in delivering an "engaging and interactive" learning experience, training in creating high quality sharable e-content and an immersion experience in creating web 2.0 tools. These opportunities need to be built in within the academic calendar and substantiated with awards and certification to motivate teachers in learning and equipping themselves with these skills. Heads of schools will also benefit from learning the use of technology in schools, they can provide a clear and effective direction in planning and administration.

C. Pre-service training courses (B.Ed.) and their curriculum should be equipped with adequate e-learning component and must have provision for equipping prospective teachers in the use of technology resources in classroom teaching. The national policy may prescribe a leadership role for

NCTE, SCERT and other State Government agencies to help in the development of relevant curriculum.

Emphasising learning over content delivery is to be focused. Developing new learning metrics to measure student learning should be undertaken. The current system of evaluation of student learning does not allow creativity, innovation and research, which are important tools for life long learning. Learning mechanisms that promote mastery or deep learning, facilitate personalised learning based on learning styles and meta cognition can be adopted if teacher training curriculums accept new age technology tools to assess and evaluate student achievement on the basis of learning and not rote memorization. Train teachers to encourage cooperative and team learning environments.

Efforts have to be made to create a pool of effective master trainers. There should be a mechanism for scaling up the quality of training to reach the approximately seven million teachers across the country to integrate ICT in education by developing models based on case studies, experience sharing and by organising discussion groups (online and offline).

A. Relevant education bodies may be mandated with the task of developing separate ICT enabled course curriculum and e-content for different levels of school education-primary, upper primary, secondary and upper secondary.
B. Multiple mechanisms for teacher training can be used such as: Face to face workshops, self-learning and distance learning. Edusat can still be used effectively. Keeping in view the accessibility issues of the country, Radio and television should be used for both teacher training and delivery of lessons.

Digital divide is about access to, and familiarity, with technology. Teachers should have assured access to technology and resources. Provision of One Laptop Per Teacher (OLPT) should be made on a permanent basis. Computers are to be provided for staff rooms in each school. Infrastructure is an important point of intervention to bring ICT in schools. There is a need to look at appropriate software, tools and mechanism that are teacher-friendly and meet their needs in local circumstances.

There is a strong need to develop minimum standards for Instructional Design competence, standards for deployment of ICTs in teaching. These minimum standards can guide educators on effectively and innovatively use the new technology tools that focus on learning activities, rather than content delivery or general learner management. Along with these, minimum standards for student evaluation and for maintenance and management of ICT systems should also be developed. In this regard, an open ended approach may be preferred to encourage innovative outcomes.

Public-Private-Partnership can be encouraged to meet several gaps within the existing infrastructure and for scaling up measures.

Motivation in teachers is of paramount importance and there is a need to allow space and flexibility for the teachers to discover and explore the possibilities of integrating ICT in education. This will ensure buy in and ownership of educators in integrating ICTs in education.

The trainings and performance may be linked with incentives like promotions, awards, etc. This will enhance the morale of teachers and ensure their ownership in the change process.

Towards a Policy on ICT in Education

The International Conference on Universal Quality School Education (UQSE) GeSCI Session held on 23 November, 2007, at Hotel Ashok, New Delhi. The participants are:

- Osama Manzar, Digital Empowerment Foundation (DEF)
- Anshul Sonak, INTEL
- Radha Ganesan, QUEST
- Alliance Douglas Bell, Education Development Centre (EDC)
- Ajay Kapur, Oracle

Recommendations

The International Conference on Universal Quality School Education (UQSE) was organised in New Delhi by Educational Technology and management Academy, in association with UNICEF, UNESCO, and Media Lab Asia. The conference was attended by a number of academicians, educationists and experts from across various sectors that included Schools, corporate, non-government and government. The session elaborated on the role of technology in leveraging school education and emphasised on the need to have a guiding policy at state/ district level to solve the complexities of implementing ICT in school education.

Recommendations

- *Learner-centric Policy:* The country has a young demography and the policy should support the learners and empower them with 21st century skill sets to build an efficient workforce for the knowledge economy.
- *Innovation:* ICT can act as a catalyst in achieving education for all through innovative uses of technology in the education system. The community should be empowered to bring in innovation in the adoption and use of ICT across the country. ICT should not be just about computers. It should support knowledge creation at local level.
- *Strengthening of Dialogue:* The policy should support the two-way process of dialogues, which includes the top-down model from the states-to-villages and the bottom-up model of villages/grassroots initiatives being incorporated and recognised by the state. There should be a technology-people connection.
- *Infrastructure Standards:* There is a need to identify and outline the ICT infrastructure requirements of a school for adoption of technology for teaching and learning. There is a need to outline the role of school management on ICT decisions in schools. The connectivity benchmarks should be laid down for schools.
- *Instructional Design:* The content should be based on instructional design and pedagogical instructions. The infrastructure component should consider the hardware/ software solutions on using digital content for teaching and learning.
- *Need Analysis for School-Survey:* There is a need to research and execute a survey methodology for identifying the ICT needs of schools for adoption of ICT in teaching and learning.
- *Setting of Targets:* There is a need to set targets for adoption of ICT in schools.
  - 5 yrs–10 yrs. computer literacy or Internet literacy should be attained after schooling.
  - The target attainment of Computer: Student ratio in the next years.
- *Professional Development of Teachers:* The role of teachers should be defined in the policy and ICT to support the teacher should be outlined and should not aim to replace the teacher.

Pre and in-service teachers should be given priority for capacity building and teacher training to introduce the IT skill sets for teachers.

- *B.Ed. Curriculum:* The policy should suggest a change of the B.Ed. curriculum of institutes of teacher training to include ICT as a compulsory component. There should be teacher competency standards laid down in the policy.
- *ICT for Girl Education:* The policy should initiate and support projects and programmes to use ICTs for maximising the education reach to the girl child empowering them for a brighter future and skilled workforce.
- *Radio – An Introductory Technology:* The innovative use of radio as an introductory technology will provide an opportunity for the schools to start on an ICT roadmap. Radio being cost-effective and high penetration across all rural areas should be promoted as a technology tool for education outreach.
- *Introduction of Internet-based Research:* Connectivity is bringing knowledge exchange and changing interactions nation-wide, knowledge sharing is now two-way global-local. The policy should address issues of connectivity and account for the availability of resources and time to utilise this important learning tool.
- *ICT Advocacy:* The government needs to be aware of the issues of ICT technology and its benefits in the education sector. There is a need for strong ICT advocacy by NGOs, CSOs and other organisations working in the domain of ICT and education. The States should adopt a leadership role.
- *Financial Assistance:* The policy should allocate the financial outlay for ICT in education programmes as we face lack of funds.
- *Content Quality Standards:* There is a need to lay down the quality standards on using ICT in education for quality content reaching our classrooms.
- *Co-ordination of Policies:* There is a diversity of policies; hence the policy should be in co-ordination with all.
- *Building Strong PPP:* The policy should create a PPP friendly environment for the initiation and implementation of ICT in education projects in India. A good PPP – a larger dialogue of all stakeholders for appropriate mechanism at excellence at all levels: Top-down and bottom-up mechanism.

- Monitoring and Evaluation of ICT projects and programmes in the education is required through setting up of an agency within or outside the government. It should also monitor the quality of digital content provided into schools.
- *Content Development*: The development of content should be supported by both private providers and community/ teachers to progress towards a paradigm-shift of content for school education.
- *Scalability of Pilots:* The successful pilot projects should be promoted to be scalable at the district/state level for implementation.

MODEL QUESTIONS

1. How ICT made change in School Curriculum?
2. What you mean by 'Digital divide'?
3. How ICT useful for teachers?
4. What is the role of the organizations like NCERT and NCTE regarding capacity-building of schools and teachers in ICT?

REFERENCES

1. http://digitallearning.in/articles/article-details.asp?articleid policymatters
2. http://www.csdms.in/gesci/nc-detail.asp
3. http://www.csdms.in/gesci/r-detail.asp

17

Important Websites on Education

Introduction

In this chapter a list of important websites in the field of education has been given. This list includes educational institutions, academic bodies, studies abroad, job opportunities abroad, online libraries, books, educational research, teaching resources, learning materials, information sites and so on.

LIST OF WEBSITES

Books

www.amazon.com

www.authorsshop.com

www.books-online.com

www.booxop.com

www.bibliomania.com

www.esmarts.com/books

www.fabmart.com

www.powells.com

www.schandgroup.com

Educational Institutions

www.aiuweb.org

www.annamalaiuniversity.ac.in

www.goodschoolsofindia.com

www.madrasuniversity.org

www.mkuniv.org

www.tamilnadueducation.com

www.tnuniv.ac.in/annmalai

www.tnuniv.ac.in

www.uni-info.com

www.velscollege.com

www.xl.webcom/heritage/asian

E-Learning

www.acelearner.com

www.aptechonlinevarsity.com

www.blackboard.com

www.brainvisa.com

www.computeraccess.co.in/sanskrutavj

www.digitalthink.com

www.educationbangalore.com

www.eduwrite.com

www.egurucool.com

www.elementk.com

www.elearn2excel.com

www.hp.com/e-learning

www.ivlu.com

www.iitpl.com

www.learnenglish.org/uk

www.learningbyte.com

www.lifelonglearning.com

www.mySAP.com

www.msonline.com

www.netvarsity.com

www.piewebtutor.com

www.zeelearn.com

Employment

www.1-jobs.com
www.6figurejobs.com
www.alltimejobs.com
www.ajb.dnj.us
www.bankjobs.com
www.bestjobsusa.com
www.computerjobs.com
www.careerjobs.com
www.careersit.com
www.careers.com
www.emergencyjobs.com
www.engineeringjobs.com
www.education.nic.in
www.fpjobs.com
www.gotojob.com
www.hoteljobs.com
www.jobsabroad.com
www.lawjobs.com
www.manpower.com
www.naukari.com
www.nationjob.com

Encyclopaedia/Dictionary

www.encyclopaedia.com
www.nupedia.com
www.yourdictionary.com

English Speaking

www.fleunzy.om
www.mindpowerindia.com
www.learningenglish.org.uk.

E-Zines and E-Journals

www.ambalam.com
www.chennaionline.com
www.hinduonline.com
www.india.connect.com
www.mediatreks.com
www.webulagam.com
www.wsj.com
www.zdnet.com
www.experimentsineducation.150m.com
www.innovationsinindianeducation.150m.com
www.educationnews.150m.com

Indian Languages

www.bengalimail.com
www.gujaratmail.com
www.hindipatra.com
www.malayalipathram.com
www.oriyamail.com
www.tamilanjal.com
www.telugulekha.com

Information

www.ciol.com
www.galatta.com
www.infexchange.com
www.jayahey.com
www.kamat.com
www.yet2.com

Internet Counselling

www.lifetechno.com

Internet Libraries

www.books-on-line.com
www.bibliomania.com

http://books-mirror.org

www.esmarts.com/books

www.inflibnet.ernet.in

www.showare.com

www.w3.org/hypertext/data/sources/bysubject

Online Varsity

www.classesontheweb.com

www.jobstreet.com

www.onlinevarsity.com

Overseas Employment

www.careerpath.com

www.discindia.com

www.overseasjobs.net

www.londoncareers.net

www.usajobs.com

Research Scholars in Education

www.academicresearch.com

www.dissertation.com

www.experimentsineducation.150m.com

www.innovationsinindianeducation.150m.com

Search Engines

www.altavista.digital.com

www.aol.com/netfind

www.askjeeves.com

www.coolnords.com/search

www.excite.com

www.god.co.uk

www.goto.com

www.google.com

www.hotbot.com

www.infoseek.com

www.inktomi.com

www.lycos.com

www.lookssmart.com

www.lastech.com

www.netscape.com

www.netguide.com

www.netcom.com

www.opentext.com

www.snap.com

www.snoopie.com

www.yahoo.com

Search Engines for Children

www.aol.com/netfind/kinds

www.disney.go.com/dig/today

www.jumbo.com/pags/kids

www.weberawler.com/ckv

www.yahoolligans.com

Students Sites

www.brainvisa.com

www.careerlauncher.com

www.careerrange.com

www.ecolloge.com

www.earnwhilelearn.com

www.gomath.com

www.marksheet.com

www.sturoit.com

www.stamath.com

www.thinkwave.com

www.tutor.com

www.tripod.com

Ministries and National Bodies

Ministry of Human Resource Development

www.education.nic.in

University Grants Commission

www.ugc.ac.in

All India Council of Technical Education

www.aicte.ernet.in

National Council of Teacher Education

www.ncte.in.org

Association of Indian Universities

www.aiuweb.org

Medical Council of India

www.mciindia.org

Distance Education Council

www.dec.ac.in

MODEL QUESTION

Visit any four educational websites and prepare a analytical report.

REFERENCE

Rajasekar, S. (2004). *Computer Education and Educational Computing*. Hyderabad: Neelkamal Publications (P) Ltd.

Bibliography

Abdu, V.K. (1999). *Computer Lokam (Malayalam)*. Kozhikode: IPH.

Alan Han Cock, *Planning for Educational Mass Media*. London: Longman.

Arora, A. *A Complete Book on B.Ed. Information Technology*. New Delhi: Cyber Tech Publications.

BBC News Article "Families Enrol for Online School."

Blurton, C.,"New Directions of ICT-Use in Education." Available online http://www.unesco.org/education/educprog/lwf/dl/edict.pdf.

Briteschool FAQ "Disadvantages of Attending an Online School."

Chandra, R. (2005). *Technology Integration in Education*. Delhi: Kalpaz Publications.

Daniel, J.S. (1996). *Mega-Universities and Knowledge Media: Technology Strategies for Higher Education*, Kogan Page, London.

Das, S.K. (2005). *A Textbook of Information Technology*. New Delhi: Dominant Publishers and Distributors.

Dorveaux, Xavier (2007-07-15). "Apprendre une langue dans un monde virtuel", Le Monde. Retrieved on 15 July 2007.

Emery: Edwin *et. al.*, (1987). *Introduction to Mass-Communication*. Vakil, Preffer and Simens (Pvt.).

EnGauge. North Central Regional Educational Laboratory; available from http://www.ncrel.org/engauge/skills/21skills.htm.

Goel, H.K. *Teaching of Computer Science*. Meerut: R. Lall Book Depot.

Gold, L. & Maitland, C. (1999). What's the Difference? A Review of Contemporary Research on the Effectiveness of Distance Learning in Higher Education. Washington, DC: NEA.

Government of Kerala, Department of Education (2007). *Information Technology*-I, Thiruvananthapuram.

Hebert, D.G. (2007). "Five Challenges and Solutions in Online Music Teacher Education," Research and Issues in Music Education, Vol. 5.

Holmberg, B. (2005). *The Evolution, Principles and Practices of Distance Education*. Bibliotheks-und Informations system der Universitat Oldenburg.

Hoole, H.S. *et al.*, (2005). *Information and Communication Technology for Teachers*. New Delhi: Foundation Books.

http://derekstockley.com.au/elearning-definition

http://digitallearning.in/articles/article-details.asp?articleid policymatters

http://en.wikipedia.org/wiki/Distance_education

http://en.wikipedia.org/wiki/Education

http://en.wikipedia.org/wiki/E-learning

http://en.wikipedia.org/wiki/Information_ communication_ technology#PC-based_ICT

http://en.wikipedia.org/wiki/Information_ communication_ technology

http://en.wikipedia.org/wiki/Information_technology

http://en.wikipedia.org/wiki/Virtual_education

http://en.wikipedia.org/wiki/Virtual_school

http://lyon.chin.gc.ca/.../module3

http://searchciomidmarket.techtarget.com/sDefinition/0,,sid183_ gci928405,00. html

http://www.csdms.in/gesci/nc-detail.asp

http://www.csdms.in/gesci/r-detail.asp

http://www.educ.utas.edu.au/.../thesis/html/design

http://www.htk.tlu.ee/TLG/strategy/masterplan2

http://www.ignou.ac.in

http://www.ignou.ac.in. See also Asian Development Bank (1997), *Distance Education for Primary School Teachers: Papers and Proceedings of the Regional Seminar on Distance Education* (Manila:Asian Development Bank).

http://www.mission_india.org

http://www.open.ac.uk

http://www.webopedia.com/TERM/d/distance_learning

International Center for Distance Learning, "Universitas Terbuka/ Indonesian Open Learning University"; available from http://www-icdl.open.ac.uk/instResult.ihtml?inst_id Victoria L. Tinio,ICT in *Education.*

International Labour Organization, "Learning and Training for Work in the Knowledge Society;" available from http://www.Ilo.org/public/ English/employment/skills/recomm/report.

Jain, V.K. (2001). *Computer for Beginners.* Delhi: Pustak Mahal.

Jean Piaget Society. 2001. URL: http://www.piaget.org.

"Key Facts", University of London External Programme Website, http://www.londonexternal.ac.uk/about_us/facts.

Khvilon, E. & Patru, M. (2002). Information and Communication Technologies in Teacher Education, A Planning Guide, UNESCO Division of Higher Education.

Kurbel, Karl: Virtuality on the Students' and on the Teachers' Sides: A Multimedia and Internet based International Master Programme; ICEF Berlin GmbH (Eds.), Proceedings on the 7th International Conference on Technology Supported Learning and Training—Online Educa; Berlin, Germany; November 2001, pp. 133–136.

Lave, J. 1988. Cognition in Practice: Mind, Mathematics, and Culture in Everyday Life. Cambridge, UK: Cambridge University Press. In Lave, J., & Wenger, E. 1990. *Situated Learning: Legitimate Peripheral Participation.* Cambridge, UK: Cambridge University Press.

Loutchko, Iouri; Kurbel, Karl; Pakhomov, Alexei: Production and Delivery of Multimedia Courses for Internet Based Virtual Education; The World Congress "Networked Learning in a Global Environment: Challenges and Solutions for Virtual Education", Berlin, Germany, May 1-4, 2002.

Malhan, P.N. (1985). *Communication Media Yesterday, Today and Tomorrow.* Ministry of Information and Broadcasting. New Delhi: Government of India.

Mallik, U. (2002). *Learning with Computers*. New Delhi: NCERT.

Mcqual, D. (1987). *Mass Communication Theory*. Sage Publication.

Merriam, S., Caffarella, R., & Baumgartner, L. (2007). Learning in Adulthood New York: Wiley.

Moore, Michael G.; Greg Kearsley (2005). *Distance Education: A Systems View*, Second, Belmont, CA: Wadsworth.

NEC TEC. (July 2002) *ICT for Poverty Reduction*: Examples of Programmes/Projects in Thailand.

Newby, T., Stepich, D., Lehman, J., and Russel, J. 2000. *Instructional Technology for Teaching and Learning*. Upper Saddle River, Merrill/Prentice Hall, New Jersey: National School Board Association. 2002. *Why Change?*: http://www.nsba.org/sbot/toolkit/WhyChange.html

Nochad, A. & Shanavas. *Information and Communication Technology*. Calicut University: Shaan Vishaal.

Oshima, J., Bereiter, C., and Scardamalia, M. 1995. Information-Access Characteristics for High Conceptual Progress in a Computer-Networked Learning Environment. In *Proceedings CSCL'95 (Computer Support for Collaborative Learning) Conference*.

Parker, Quin (2007-04-06). "A Second Look at School Life", The Guardian. Retrieved on 16 June 2007.

Pathak, G.P. (2005). *Education and Communication Technology*. New Delhi: Reference Press.

Postman, N. 1969. *Teaching as a Subversive Activity*. Doubleday, New York.

Prasad, K. (Ed.) (2004). *Information and Communication Technology: Recasting Development*. Delhi: B.R. Publishing Corporation.

Pribram, K. 1991. *Brain and Perception: Holonomy and Structure in Figural Processing Lawrence Erlbaum*, Mahwah, New Jersey.

Proceedings of World Academy of Science, Engineering and Technology Volume 30 July 2008.

Pwaset Volume 30 July 2008, waset.org

Rajasekar, S. (2004). *Computer Education and* Educational *Computing*. Hyderabad: Neelkamal Publications (P) Ltd.

Raju Kumar, http://www.waset.org/pwaset

Rao, D.B. (Ed.) (2003). *Teachers in a Changing World.* New Delhi: Discovery Publishing House.

Ratnajeevan, S. *et al.*, (2005). *ICT for Teachers.* New Delhi: Foundation Books.

Resta, P. 1996. *Technology and Changing Views of the Learning Process.* Texas School Boards Association Journal. 11 (8).

Salomon, G. (Ed.). 1993. *Distributed Cognitions: Psychological and Educational Considerations.* Cambridge University Press.

Sethumadhavan, P. *Internet Oru Padanam* (Malayalam). Calicut: Lipi Publications.

Singh, J. & Singh, K. *Computer Education.* Ludhiana: Tandon Publications.

The Commonwealth of Learning, "An Introduction to Open and Distance Learning"; available from http://www.col.org/ODLIntro/introODL.htm.

U.K. Singh and K.N. Sudarshan, *Media Education.*

US Department of Labour (1999), *Futurework-Trends and Challenges for Work in the 21st Century.*

White, M. (1982). 'Distance Education in Australian Higher Education – A History', *Distance Education,* Vol. 3, Issue 2.

World Bank (1998), *The World Development Report 1998/99. Quoted in Blurton, C., New Directions of ICT-Use in Education.*

Index